The
POWER
OF Positive
Doing

D1469147

The
POWER
OF +++♥+++ Positive
Doing
By
IVAN BURNELL

A publication of

INTERNATIONAL PERSONAL DEVELOPMENT

Second Printing 1994

The Power of Positive Doing
by Ivan G. Burnell

Library of Congress Catalog Card Number:
90-80402

ISBN No. 0-9625806-0-0

Contents

Acknowledgment

I wish to express my heartfelt thanks to the many International Personal Development clients and YES Course graduates who graciously consented for me to use their no-holds-barred comments and introspective stories throughout the book.

Author's Preface

Positive Doing

Life is not a spectator activity:

A spectator is a person who reacts to an event that has already occurred. Whatever the reaction — positive or negative — is how the spectator interprets the event.

The only way to control an event is to participate in it.

Being a participant requires a great deal of effort, but eventually the benefits will far exceed the efforts.

After all, being a spectator also requires effort, but the benefits are over when the event is finished. Because you contributed nothing, you receive nothing which lasts.

Be good to yourself — participate in life!

—GIL ADAMS
YES Graduate

Positive Doing Means . . .

Positive thinking, popularized since mid-century, has changed thousands of lives for the better. On that, no one can argue. The greatest scholars and teachers throughout history — from Ptolemy to Jesus Christ, and from Ralph Waldo Emerson to Norman Vincent Peale — have all agreed on this one point: You are what you allow inside your mind.

Positive talking (self-affirmation), which became more accepted during the Seventies, has fueled many, many people toward happiness and success. Every person who is successful has learned to achieve lofty goals by giving himself or herself positive pep-talks. Conversely, every person who wallows in failure is an expert at negative self-talk. This is a universal principle.

The Power of Positive Doing builds on the foundations of positive thinking and talking. More importantly, this book takes a bold step forward by offering business people, professionals and individuals a nuts-and-bolts set of workable strategies for accomplishing whatever that person wants to do in all areas of life: career, financial, intimacy, relationships, spiritual, recreation and family.

Creating Step-By-Step Success

I spent many years as an engineer, working part of that time with NASA, and since I am still an engineer at heart, this book is quite different from most others written to build personal and professional development. Engineers tend to think in very practical, pragmatic terms.

I have taught these principles for nearly three decades, and the classes that I teach have evolved into a series called the YES Course. The Power of Positive Doing came to life as a result of a growing number of requests from those who attended the 10-session course.

Using thousands of those previous students as examples, I can wholeheartedly say that *you will achieve any success you desire if you are willing to do the work outlined in the following chapters — step by step.*

In working with both the corporate and private sector, I never cease to be amazed at the large number of people who *think* about fulfillment and *talk* about achievement, yet the few who want to *do* anything about it.

Certainly, it is easier to complain, to be a perpetual victim of bad luck or to buy an endless array of lottery tickets, always hoping to finally become incredibly rich or happy. Why should you live that way?

You deserve better than that. With these guidelines for living, you will learn that life is so much more than looking backward or preparing for the future.

The past is important, and you should never neglect the future, but you must learn to live this moment. Life is right now! Success begins this instant.

You don't have to spend your life saying, "It will be great when . . ." or "Things will be better just as soon as I . . ." or other happiness-is-just-around-the-corner phrases.

There is a better way!

No Matter What You Face

The Power of Positive Doing offers you tools in a number of areas: inner importance, honesty, negative blockages, goal-setting, your mind-switch, anger, love, intuition, self-talk and giving.

I will help you sharpen these tools by offering a Positive Doing Insights section in each chapter so that you can begin internalizing the truths you are learning. And you can review the main points of each chapter in a Positive Steps page.

But how long will it take for you to transform these tools into life-changing disciplines?

A more appropriate question is this: How long did it take to get where you are today?

You are on a path, and if you want to change your direction, it will take forever, one step at a time.

After all, success is a journey. The path goes on as long as you have breath.

Do these principles work in the marketplace?

Glenn Freeman, a district manager with the United States Department of the Interior, has written:

> "I want to thank you for the Yes Course. I have participated in several manager development seminars. None of them has come close to providing the comprehensive program in YES I and II. The personal management tools you provide are straightforward, workable, and extremely effective."

Bob and Terry Wentworth, well-known restaurant owners, wrote these words in a recent letter:

> "Over the past six months, Ivan Burnell has been helping us build a strong working team.

Because of the tools they have given us to use, we have an excited, interested group of employees who genuinely like coming to work. Ivan has integrated programs that benefit our business. Our turnover in labor has shown a definite decrease and the quality of new employees has increased. We strongly recommend The Power of Positive Doing and International Personal Development to any business which is concerned with the quality of service, production and morale."

Dave Byerly, general manager of a Montana-based publishing company, took the YES Course, then had each of his department heads take it. He says:

"This has had a definite and positive impact on our company. The improved attitudes, personal relations techniques and problem-solving skills of our leaders have been reflected through the entire company. The improvement in employee attitude and motivation has been noticeable. The numbers, in terms of production and profit, speak very clearly."

Marcia Appleton, a retail manager for a Northeast company, says:

"I have grown significantly, both personally and professionally. I have learned to take responsibility for my own actions. My life has changed drastically since I started setting true goals. And in the business arena, my confidence has gone up considerably. I realized that by working on myself and by changing myself from the inside, I could succeed at anything. As a result, I have been able to accept and approve of others better. That has made me a better manager."

Can these personal and professional changes begin happening to you and the people in your company? Only you can answer that question.

Ageless Principles

What I will share with you is hardly new. Success principles have been around forever. They don't change. But the fact is that few people recognize these coded strategies. Fewer yet understand them.

I will present these ageless principles in a new way. Not many management consultants talk about green gorillas, peeled onions, staked elephants or pole-climbing.

You will be encouraged to learn by your experience, of course; more importantly, you will be challenged to learn through a better perception of those experiences. There is a major difference! Too often we learn the wrong thing from our experiences. You can change that pattern.

A Final Note

You can have whatever you want! If you want negative things, there are plenty of negatives which will come your way. If, however, you want positive things to happen, you can learn to make the right choices.

You do not have to be a victim your entire life. What you are right now is a result of past choices. What you become will be directly related to the choices you make from now on.

Take a moment to think about your own success. If you could have anything you wanted — right at this moment — what would it be? Be more specific than just "I'd like to be happy." What would you like your life to be like? Take the time to write your answers in a notebook.

Finished?

Take heart. In the decades of teaching my YES Courses and management consulting, I have never heard anyone's definition of success that couldn't be achieved through the principles you will uncover in The Power of Positive Doing. This has been true for CEOs to chicken farmers, salespeople to frontline workers and professionals to parents.

You can have whatever you want in every area of your life if you use The Power of Positive Doing!

Positive +++♥++ *Steps*

(1) The Power of Positive Doing takes a bold step forward by offering a practical set of tools for accomplishing whatever a person wants to do in life.

(2) You can move from knowledge into understanding and wisdom. Knowledge without understanding produces negativism and discontent.

(3) Your choices will decide your destiny.

You want success 1
How much?

In times of change, learners inherit the earth, while the learned find themselves beautifully equipped to deal with a world that no longer exists.

—ERIC HOFFER

I understand that I am responsible for who I am.
I understand that I am responsible for what I am.
I understand that when I am responsible, I can be whomever and whatever I choose.

—MATTHEW MACDONALD
YES Graduate

Questions

John Sculley is the former Pepsi-Cola executive who engineered the highly-publicized, mid-80s turnaround of Apple Computer. In his autobiography Sculley wrote:

"Visionaries are constantly fighting conventional wisdom because they see the world ahead in terms of what it can be if someone is willing to look at things in very different ways."[1]

This book is for visionaries — people who are willing to ask questions, to be innovative and to view the world through inquiring eyes.

The ancient Greeks knew that "the unexamined life is not worth living." Over the Temple at Delphi the words were inscribed: KNOW THYSELF. They knew the importance of self-knowledge and self-inquiry as the keys to all other knowledge.

Pythagoras, one of the greatest mathematics and philosophy teachers in ancient Greece, demanded that every night his pupils examine themselves on that day's progress. They were to ask themselves these questions:

"How did I succeed in my studies today?"

"Could I have learned more?"

"Could I have studied better?"

"Is there something I neglected?"

As a result of these self-inquiries, all of the master's students became well-known for their learning abilities.

---

1. John Sculley, *Odyssey: Pepsi to Apple . . . A Journey of Adventure, Ideas and the Future* (New York: Harper & Row, 1987), p. 23.

The Power of Positive Doing

Questions! If you reflect on the greatest, most progressive, highly successful people who have lived throughout history, you will see that they were universally better at asking questions than unsuccessful men and women. The same is true today. The best-known CEOs, corporate fast-trackers and achieving entrepreneurs are highly proficient questioners.

George Bernard Shaw echoed this need for questions when he wrote, "Some men see things as they are and say, 'Why?' I dream things that never were and say, 'Why not?'"

This importance of questions — what does this mean for you?

A Different View of the Corporate World

Ralph Waldo Emerson used to recognize old friends whom he had not seen in a while with the following question: "What's become clear to you since we've last met?"

Emerson's question is one which can be invaluable to ask *yourself* at various mileposts in your life.

I have, and as a businessman, management consultant and engineer and educator, there are many things which have become clear to me through the years.

At 11, I began working at my first summer job, doing a grown man's work, in a coal and ice house on Long Island. At the tender age of 19, less than a year out of high school, I was named supervisor of a manufacturing department within an electronics firm. After returning to college and serving in the army during the

Korean Conflict, I continued my career in industrial engineering and management. During the early stages of the Saturn rocket and manned space flights, I reached an engineering apex — consulting with NASA.

The past 30 years of my life have been spent in management consulting, creativity, personal/professional development, and field training. My International Personal Development clients include large-, middle- and small-sized companies, as well as individual seminar attendees from all over the nation and several foreign countries.

From this work, I have developed the YES Course, an intensive ten-session study of personal and professional development. Thousands of people have taken these classes.

Along the way, many things have become quite clear — Emerson-wise — to me. For starters, my research shows that most people do not feel very fulfilled, happy or successful.

Today, American employees admit working at less than half their capacity. A majority have no stated purpose for being employed other than making money to live. A recent Roper Report, based on interviews with 2,000 American adults, said that only a third believe their job is interesting.[2]

As low as one-fourth of all corporate leaders indicate that they know how to be sensitive to others or how to build a loyal team. Too many frontline, middle and topline managers continue to fail largely because they are frustrated at being expected to motivate people with unclear or constantly-changing objectives.

Not surprisingly, today 77% of all American workers, from frontline employees to top management, say

---

2. Web Bryant, "Dreaming of the Good Life," *USA Today,* April 4, 1989, p. D1.

that they are actively looking, or thinking of looking, for another job.[3]

That same level of transience and discontent permeates every level of our society. More than half of us drift in and out of long-term relationships on an average of every four years. Too many children are growing into adults without a sense of purpose or responsibility.

Why?

We have more education and knowledge available today than ever before. Opportunities abound for workplace excellence and achievement. Thousands of "boat people" and immigrants continue to prove that this is the ultimate land of opportunity for those who understand The Power Of Positive Doing.

Discontent is not bad if it brings positive changes, but discontent that breeds a negative attitude can be catastrophic on any life-level.

There is a better way — one that involves a number of questions.

A Positive Outlook

After more than 30 years in the marketplace, I believe, more strongly than ever, that we should be the most fulfilled, happy, strong-willed, mission-minded people in the history of our planet. Despite admitted negative influences in the world, I know that every person who is alive today can be incredibly successful, provided they are given the proper knowledge and are able to understand The Power Of Positive Doing.

---

3. Frank Grazian, "What Do These Bosses Lack?" *Communication Briefings,* Volume 8, Number 2, p. 3

Call me simple or naive, if you desire, but I believe that we have grossly complicated personal and professional development. We keep trying to reduce the pursuit of wisdom to a basic set of cliches and quick-fix solutions. Life just doesn't work that way. Success involves asking many, many questions.

Here is one of the most important . . .

What Do You Really Want?

Everyone has knowledge. We suffer from a knowledge glut. On any given day we must process approximately 70,000 pieces of information.

But there are millions of people around the world who, though they overflow with knowledge, continue to be unhappy, unfulfilled, self-sabotaging and unsuccessful. Why?

Knowledge without understanding produces negative results and discontent, and you cannot gain understanding without questions.

Most students can memorize by rote and parrot enough correct answers to satisfy teachers, but relatively few students or teachers understand the true educational process. Likewise, most business people can function knowledgeably throughout life, but a scant few are willing to pay the price for true understanding and wisdom.

Are you intent on obtaining knowledge or are you looking for understanding?

Your answer to that question will determine your destiny.

A SELF-TEST

Let me suggest that you obtain a spiral notebook which you can use while reading The Power Of Positive Doing. You will have a number of opportunities to write your thoughts or answer specific questions, beginning with this Self-Test.

In that notebook, write a complete sentence for each of the following phrases. Work rapidly, writing down the first thing that pops into your mind.

(1)   More than anything, I want:

(2)   My life is:

(3)   I hope I can:

(4)   I have achieved:

(5)   The most hopeless thing is:

(6)   The whole purpose of my life is:

(7)   I get bored when/if:

(8)   Death is:

(9)   People are:

(10)   I am accomplishing:

(11)   Illness and suffering can be:

(12)   To me, all life is:

SCORING is up to you! How do you feel about your answers?
What do your sentences say about your self-esteem and hopes for
the future?

Look at your answer to the statement, "More than anything, I want _____." Whatever you wrote in that blank, may I ask, *how much* do you want it?

It is said that a young man came to Socrates one day and said, "I have walked 1,500 miles to gain wisdom and learning. I want learning, so I came to you. Can you give it to me?"

Socrates said, "Come, follow me."

The well-known teacher led the way down to the seashore. He waded out into the water until he and his young follower were in water up to their waists.

Then Socrates seized his companion and forced his head under the water. In spite of the younger man's violent struggles, the teacher held him under.

Finally, when most of the resistance was gone, Socrates pulled the young man out of the water, laid his would-be student on the shore and returned to the marketplace.

When the young man regained his strength, he returned to Socrates.

"You are a man of learning and wisdom," the young man protested angrily. "Why did you treat me so horribly?"

"When you were under the water," Socrates asked, "what was the one thing you wanted more than anything else?"

"I wanted air!"

Then Socrates said, "When you want wisdom and understanding as badly as you wanted air, you won't have to ask anyone to give it to you. You will get it wherever and whenever you can!"

What Do You Want?

Questions — how much do you want the answers? What, exactly, do you want out of life? How badly do you want wisdom, understanding or _____?

The Power Of Positive Doing offers you more than a collection of answers. In this book you will find a set of proven tools with which you can sharpen your questioning and answering power!

On the following pages you will read information which can help change your life. Everyday I receive letters from people who have been helped by my YES Courses or International Personal Development systems.

This book, however, won't do anything for you unless you are willing to put the knowledge to use in your life. I will provide numerous exercises, but those life-changers are mere black words on white paper until you process that information inwardly. That processing requires questioning and looking deep inside yourself.

That, in a paragraph, is the difference between The Power Of Positive Doing and so many other worthwhile programs. You will be shown, step by step, how to integrate and intensify these action-based strategies.

This isn't a book about psychology, philosophy, morals, ethics, -isms or -ologies. It is simply a very down-to-earth kind of book that shows you how life really works and how you can get the most out of it.

A Final Note

Questions! Become a great asker of questions. Rudyard Kipling once wrote:

"I had six honest serving men —
  they taught me all I knew:
Their names were Where and What and When —
  and Why and How and Who."

"To take the leaps?" asked James F. Bandrowski, president of Strategic Management Associates (referring to "leaps" in terms of personal or professional development), "A provocative question is the only way I've found."[4]

Most people are afraid to ask questions. They are afraid they will appear stupid or unlearned. It relates to a lack of confidence. That is why, in my management consulting work and during all YES Course sessions, I make sure that a lot of questions are asked.

Questions! Ask yourself, "How much do I want to succeed?" That is the first strategy in The Power Of Positive Doing as you move toward getting control of your life.

---

4. Michael Ray and Rochelle Myers, *Creativity in Business* (New York: Doubleday, 1986), p. 67.

Positive +++♥++ *Steps*

---

(1) The greatest, most progressive, highly successful people who have lived throughout history were universally better at asking questions.

(2) Discontent is not bad if it brings positive changes, but discontent that breeds negative feelings can be catastrophic on any life-level.

(3) Every person who is alive today can be incredibly successful, provided they are given the proper knowledge and are able to understand The Power Of Positive Doing.

There are 2
—No Accidents

How I think
          determines
What I think
          determines
My attitude
          determines
What I do
          determines
My environment
          reinforces
How I think.

And the cycle starts all over again.

—DAGNY BURNELL
YES Instructor

What Do You Want From Life?

Mike Endicott, a YES Course graduate, wrote these revealing words in a recent letter:

"The fear of making changes doesn't stand in my way anymore. Today I find that my energy is used more efficiently to maintain my life rather than revolutionize it, yet I am still making important changes, exciting ones. For the first time in my 39 years, when someone asks me what I'm going to be when I grow up, I have an answer. I like that!"

How about you? If you could have whatever you want, what would it be? What would your life be like? Would you desire:

Peace of mind?

To feel good about yourself?

A sense of pride?

Plenty of money?

Recognition?

A recent Roper Report poll, based on interviews with several thousand American adults, pointed to six primary "what-do-I-want-out-of-life" dreams:

• The highest percentage, 86%, wanted to *own a home*. Of those polled, 60% had attained this dream.

- The next highest number, 77%, desired *a happy marriage*, but only 55% felt that they had reached this goal.

- Less than 75% listed *owning a car* as a desire — perhaps because this is such a commonality today — and 82% already had achieved this common transaction.

- 72% wanted to have *children*, and 62% had achieved this dream.

- 62% dreamed of having *lots of money*, but only a miniscule 4% had reached that goal.

- 61% desired *an interesting job*, but only one-third of those polled felt successful in this important pursuit.[1]

What does this say about success? Everybody, it seems, wants a measure of success. People generally want what they feel life can deliver.

---

1. Web Bryant, "Dreaming of the Good Life," *USA Today,* April 4, 1989, p. D1.

Success Is Personal

Success is not easily defined. Perhaps the problem lies in semantics.

Sure, people use meaningful phrases which spotlight personal fulfillment, progress and the realization of worthwhile dreams, but when it comes to specific goals, there is so much disagreement.

To many people, success might mean having enough money to pay every bill on time, which probably is not a useful definition of success for Donald Trump or Barbra Streisand. Having a home filled with a happy family might not seem at all like success for certain fast-track, single executives.

You see, success is a very personal issue. As long as you keep defining success by outside definitions, you will be largely unfulfilled.

I believe that your definition of success must come from within. I also believe that success means that you should have a vision for reaching beyond where you are right now. But only you know what your goals and dreams include.

Where do you want to be? More importantly, where are you right now? Use the following self-test to unlock insight into yourself:

MY PURPOSE IN LIFE

For each of the following statements, select the number that would be most nearly true for you. Note that the numbers always extend from one extreme feeling to its opposite kind of feeling. "Neutral" implies no judgment either way; use this rating as little as possible.

Use your companion notebook to write your answers.

(1) I am usually:

1	2	3	4	5	6	7
completely bored			neutral		exuberant and enthusiastic	

(2) Life to me seems:

1	2	3	4	5	6	7
completely routine			neutral			always exciting

(3) In life I have:

1	2	3	4	5	6	7
no goals or aims at all			neutral		very clear goals and aims	

(4) My personal existence is:

1	2	3	4	5	6	7
Utterly empty and meaningless			neutral			very purposeful

(5) Every day is:

    1   2   3   4   5   6   7

  exactly   neutral   constantly

  the same   new and different

(6) If I could choose, I would:

    1   2   3   4   5   6   7

  prefer never   neutral   like nine

  to have been   more lives just

     born   like this one

(7) After retiring, I would:

    1   2   3   4   5   6   7

  loaf the   neutral   do some exciting

  rest of my   things I have always

    life   wanted to do

(8) In achieving life goals I have:

    1   2   3   4   5   6   7

  made no progress neutral   progressed to

    whatsoever   complete fulfillment

(9) My life is:

    1   2   3   4   5   6   7

  empty and   neutral   running over

  filled with   with exciting,

   despair   good things

(10) If I should die today, I would feel that my life has been:

    1   2   3   4   5   6   7

  completely   neutral   very

  worthless   worthwhile

(11) In thinking of my life, I:

1	2	3	4	5	6	7
often wonder why I exist			neutral			always see a reason for my being here

(12) As I view the world in relation to my life, the world:

1	2	3	4	5	6	7
completely confuses me			neutral			fits meaningfully with my life

(13) I am a:

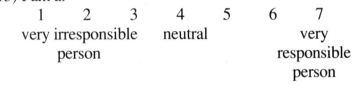

1	2	3	4	5	6	7
very irresponsible person			neutral			very responsible person

(14) Concerning freedom to make a person's own choices, I believe everyone is:

1	2	3	4	5	6	7
bound to limitations of heredity and environment			neutral			absolutely free to make all life choices

(15) With regard to death, I am:

1	2	3	4	5	6	7
unprepared and frightened			neutral			prepared and unafraid

(16) I regard my ability to find a meaning, purpose, or
     mission in life as:

     1   2   3   4   5   6   7
     practically   neutral   very great
        none

(17) My life is:

     1   2   3   4   5   6   7
     out of my hands   neutral   in my hands
     and controlled   and I am in
     by outside factors   control of it

(18) Facing my daily tasks is:

     1   2   3   4   5   6   7
     a painful and   neutral   a source of
     boring experience   pleasure and
                                          satisfaction

(19) I have discovered:

     1   2   3   4   5   6   7
     no mission   neutral   clear-cut goals
     or purpose   and a satisfying
        in life   life purpose

SCORING is determined personally. Take a few moments to examine
the reasons behind your answers. How much are you willing to change?

Changing For The Better

If you are at "X" right now, and you want to get to "Y" or "Z" (your goals), you will obviously have to make some changes in direction and attitude.

People like to think about reaching goals, but once they hear or read that phrase, "make a change," they begin to squirm. Most of us don't like change, even when it is for the better. Change can be painful, so we quickly learn to avoid it.

Look at the word: C-H-A-N-G-E. By substituting only one letter, it becomes C-H-A-N-C-E. That letter points to the difficulty in making *any* changes in life.

If you want to make a change, you are also going to have to take a chance. The greater the change, the bigger the chance.

If you are a baseball player and want to steal from first to second base, that *change* requires taking a *chance.* You can possess blistering speed and flawless sliding technique, but you also must take your foot off first base before you can advance.

If you say you want to become a millionaire, you have to accept a complex set of chances. You must commit yourself to change. You must be willing to fail.

A child learns to walk by falling down, then getting up, falling down again and rising once more. That routine is not failure; it is merely a growth process.

In using The Power of Positive Doing, you will be taking a chance. Despite the fact that this system has been a bonanza to many, many people with backgrounds and goals similar to yours, still you must be willing to change — to take a chance. You must be willing to fail without calling yourself a failure.

I hope that as the book progresses, you will be able to build change upon change, beginning with smaller, more failure-proof adjustments.

But *you* alone possess the capacity to change. If you are willing to take a chance on change, you immediately place yourself in an elite minority.

Are you willing to do that?

Scott Van Dyne was. Scott is a building contractor in the Northeast. He came to the YES Course wanting to improve his marketplace and communication skills, but also with a skeptical attitude. Scott's attitude changed. He now says:

"The most important, lasting effect was realizing that I don't have to rely on anybody else for my happiness or security. My life and my fulfillment are solely my own responsibility. At the same time, I am not responsible for anyone else's happiness. I can't tell you what that has done for my personal and professional confidence. In fact, my business has doubled since I took the course, while employing basically the same number of workers. Before, I thought I had to be the resident psychologist to motivate my employees, but I have learned that when I know exactly what I want, and when I am clear and consistent with my communication, most of the problems are taken care of. Now, I expect a lot from myself *and* my people, and — not surprisingly — I get it."

Take Responsibility

Success is no accident. Failure is no accident. Success and failure are the result of choices that you have made and actions that you have taken. In fact, there are *no* accidents!

You alone are responsible for your choices — past, present and future. You are whatever you are because of what you have allowed through your mind in the past. Moreover, you will be tomorrow whatever you choose to be because of what you allow through your mind from this moment.

Read those last two sentences out loud, personalizing the phrases:

I AM WHATEVER I AM BECAUSE OF WHAT I HAVE ALLOWED THROUGH MY MIND IN THE PAST. MOREOVER, I WILL BE TOMORROW WHATEVER I CHOOSE TO BE BECAUSE OF WHAT I ALLOW THROUGH MY MIND FROM THIS MOMENT.

This is exciting information because it is true, and because it is the key to your future.

You are responsible for your choices. The problem is this: Not all of your choices are conscious. Many times you make choices based upon subliminal perceptions and unconscious interpretations — fleeting images which can lead you astray.

Jonathan Block, a real estate manager, knew this helpless feeling very well:

"In real estate, things often seem beyond my control. You seem to be governed by the economy, by the house being too small or too large for a client, by interest rates and by financial institutions not approving mortgages. You are tempted to feel hopelessly at the whim of other people. So you 'drift.' But I have learned, using the YES tools, to focus on what I want to accomplish and I have learned how to get it. The difference is remarkable, and it has made such a contrast financially."

Before you finish reading this book, you will understand how you get what you really want and how the events in your life are planned and wanted — even those that seem detrimental at the time.

Always The Victim

You are the sum of your experiences. What you are today is a result of choices you have made in the past.

If you are not totally happy and fulfilled at the moment you read this sentence, it is because of choices that you have made in the past.

"But you don't know what it was like to have an abusive parent," seminar attenders have retorted. "How can I be a product of my choices when it was their fault?"

"I had nothing to do with the accident that disfigured my face," a client told me. "It was a drunken driver's fault, and it has affected everything I have done since that moment when he hit my car." My answer to them was, "You may or may not be in control of what happens to you, but you most assuredly are in control of how you react to what happens to you."

Regardless of the circumstances, you must accept *responsibility* (which is not the same as *blame*) for everything that has happened in your life. You must say, "I am responsible for *me*, no matter what happened, is happening or will happen."

What is the alternative to accepting responsibility for your past, your present and your future? If you do not take responsibility, then you are out of control. You have chosen to allow other people to dominate your life.

Of course, allowing other people to have control is

safe and "normal." When things go wrong, we conveniently blame parents, mates, lovers, children or bosses. Isn't that what most of us do throughout our lives?

Here is why: An overwhelming majority of the human race would rather find an excuse for failure than take a chance on becoming successful.

How about you?

A New Set of Tools

If you are willing to take a chance, to make a change for the better, accept the tools that I am offering to you.

How do these tools work?

Let's suppose for a moment that I summon two people, Ron and Tom, who are equally good at home construction. I offer Ron a crude sketch of a dwelling and hand him a *dull axe*. Then I hand Tom a detailed blueprint of a house and sharpened, precise *tools*. I point them in the direction of two stands of trees and command, "Now, build me a beautiful home."

I have no doubt, given enough time and energy, that both Ron and Tom can build me a house.

But which man will have the most satisfying product? The odds are a 100-to-1 in favor of Tom achieving the best result. Why? Highly efficient tools!

An ancient Chinese proverb states: "Never kill a fly on your forehead with an axe!" Likewise, don't use a dull or outmoded instruments to build your life. Use proper, sharpened tools.

Most people have two major problems:

(1) We don't realize that we have an unlimited array of success tools from which to choose.

(2) We don't know how to use the tools that we do know about.

Kaitlin Briggs, a management consultant, took the YES Course so that she and her husband could do something worthwhile and educational together. She says:

"Little did we know how it would change our lives. By integrating this philosophy into my life, I have been given an incredible tool kit, from which I can use different tools at different times, as the need arises. I can give a 'value structure' to my clients, since I now have this foundation for my own business. I can educate people to work with what I call the 'personal responsibility model.' When people see how they make life-affecting choices everyday, the educational process is clarified and simplified almost immediately."

Understanding and using your tools to your highest potential — that is the entire thrust of The Power of Positive Doing.

Take <u>Now</u> For An Answer

If you do begin using your tools and attaining higher levels of success, what then?

How many times have you thought:

"If only _____, I could have _____."

"I wish I would have _____."

"As soon as I get _____, I will be happy."

"When I finally do _____, my life will be what I want it to be."

Most of the human race is entrenched in yesterday's time capsules or tomorrow's time-warps. Something inside us just won't accept NOW for an answer!

Sure, yesterday is important, for it is the canvas and foundation for your life's painting. It creates your texture. Tomorrow is important, too, for it is the canvas upon which you will paint the rest of your life. Today is the most vital component, for it is only when you begin to paint vibrant colors into your life that you can begin to make a difference! It is the only time in your life that you can actually do something.

Can you accept that challenge? Are you willing to become a positive doer?

Time For You

Since you are responsible for your experiences, take a few moments — right now and during the next few days — to examine the undesirable experiences of your past. Think of accidents, for example. What was happening at that moment in your life? Were you angry at someone? (—*Think about that . . .*) What if there really were no such thing as an accident? *What if* — consciously or subconsciously — you brought those accidents into your life for some reason?

Jolene Smith, a business woman in central Montana, took a week off from her busy schedule to join her sisters as they painted their parents' house. She was chosen to paint the higher parts of the house because the others did not want to climb the ladder. After painting two sides, Jolene was smoldering. She asked her sisters again, "Would one of you mind doing the next side up-high." "No can do, sis," they answered, "'cause you know we are both afraid of heights." As she got down from the ladder and marched to the garage for more paint, she tripped on a rut and sprained her ankle.

"I certainly did not want to do that," Jolene explained later. In fact, the sprained ankle accomplished her desired end exactly. She got some rest, and her sisters overcame their fear of heights long enough to finish painting the house. Not until she took the YES Course and began examining her true thoughts was she able to see the benefits from her so-called accident.

As you begin to understand those advantages better, you will also view your "accidents" from a different perspective.

Write your thoughts in the notebook that you are using for all assignments and reflections during the remainder of The Power Of Positive Doing.

A Final Note

Success in any area of life must come through more than positive thinking or affirmative self-talk. The only road to true success is positive DOING. Doing — right now!

You see, success is something you can plant and grow throughout your life. Likewise, self-acceptance and self-importance can be nurtured and tilled.

If you don't feel good about yourself, you will reject many of the good things which come to you.

I was consulting with a large real estate company, and a salesman came to merchandise an innovative real estate video program to the two top executives of the firm to which I was consulting. The salesman launched into his presentation, which was very impressive, and before long both executives began to understand the possibilities of the program.

"I like it," one said to the video representative. "How can we put it to use?"

The salesman kept selling as though he hadn't heard the "I-like-it" phrase at all.

Within the next 20 minutes, the two executives actually told the salesman that they wanted to buy and implement his program three more times, but each time he kept "pouring it on" with more of his spiel.

Eventually he was shown to the door. Within a week the real estate company contacted a representative of a similar video selling program and contracted for mega-thousands of dollars worth of equipment and programs.

The salesman obviously had a great product and a well-developed presentation, but his battered self-esteem and expectation of failure had become chronically self-sabotaging. Undoubtedly he was a somewhat-productive salesperson, judging from his automobile and clothing, but his level of success could have been so much greater if he had known which tools to use.

Does this illustration sound far-fetched? Don't be too sure that you are free of self-sabotaging tendencies. How many times a day do you make judgements about yourself that are crippling your potential? Do you allow people to tease you or put you down? Are you a person who gets mad easily, even though you may be an expert at hiding that anger? Are you a victim, either at home with your loved ones or at work?

Take responsibility for your life right now!

Are there accidents or no accidents? Former Surgeon General C. Everett Koop told a Senate panel these revealing words:

> "People look at an accident as being a random but nevertheless inevitable event, an event ordained by fate or some other metaphysical or theological force, an event which none of us poor mortals can control in any way."[2]

---

2. "Most Injuries Preventable, Koop Claims," Associated Press, February 10, 1989

The reality, according to that report given by Koop, is that most injuries to people and nearly all injuries to children can be prevented.

Koop also said:

"We have got to convince the American people that their fatalism about accidents is unacceptable nonsense."[3]

Koop also referred to accident-fatalism as a "cop out" and a "transparent evasion of responsibility."

Once you accept the fact that there are no accidents, you can realize so much more about your true self. Within you lies a dormant, creative person waiting to be unleashed.

Take the set of tools I am offering — beginning with the concept, *you are responsible* — and begin to build or paint a lasting masterpiece.

---

3. Ibid.

Positive +++♥++ Steps

(1) Success is personal, and it can only be defined by you.

(2) C-H-A-N-G-E also involves C-H-A-N-C-E.

(3) Ask, "*What if* there are really no accidents?"

(4) You are responsible for your choices — past, present and future.

(5) If you want to build a successful life, accept the proper, sharpened tools that you are being offered.

Rule Number One 3
—You Are Important

We are all of us like newborns; with feelings and desires to grow and to be free.

We are ready for those first steps: entering non-judge-mentally into all that life can be.

We choose our self-direction each and every day; and what a wonderful choice to be happening to me.

Self-discipline is the path we follow; with absolute honesty in all our thoughts and all we see.

We allow our minds to be totally open; for there is so much to experience, don't you see?

However, most important of all is unconditional love; it is in this "state of mind" that we desire to be.
We need to fill our loving cups every day; and generously spill our love on all we meet and see.

We are yet children with desires to learn and grow; everlasting success begins with our First Steps, don't you all agree?

—DIANE THIBEAULT
YES Graduate

Rule Number One— Your Foundation

In my seminars and with my consulting clients, I emphasize the fact that a person can change his or her life by following two basic rules. The next chapter features the second guideline. Here is the first:

I AM IMPORTANT; SO IS EVERYONE ELSE.

I WILL NEVER USE MY IMPORTANCE TO PUT ANYONE DOWN.

I WILL NEVER — NEVER — *NEVER* ALLOW ANYONE TO USE THEIR IMPORTANCE TO PUT ME DOWN.

That's pretty simple, isn't it? But elementary concepts are often the most overlooked or avoided. Quoting the great broadcaster, Edward R. Murrow: "The obscure we see eventually, the completely apparent takes longer."

What have you been overlooking in your life? Use the following exercise to peer into your hidden thoughts.

INTIMATE KNOWLEDGE

Being out of touch with yourself — your true feelings and commitments — is a key contributor to frustration, burnout and failure.

"Knowing yourself" intimately is essential. To facilitate that process, let me offer the following 10 questions to ponder.

Use your companion notebook to jot down a few thoughts on as many of the following questions as possible. Don't worry if your answers are incomplete. Ask yourself:

(1) What are my greatest concerns and worries?

(2) What are the major goals that I would like to achieve during the remainder of my life?

(3) What are the most important rewards I hope to gain during my life?

(4) What are the most meaningful events I have experienced in my life?

(5) What are the major limits in my life right now which make it difficult for me to achieve the goals, rewards and experiences which I want in the future? (List several internal and external obstacles.)

(6) What are several things that I do well?

(7) What are things that I do poorly?

(8) What would I like to stop doing?

(9) What would I like to start doing or learn to do?

(10) Which part of my life (work, family, friends, self, spiritual, hobbies, etc.) is the central one right now?

SCORING — the purpose of this self-test is to clarify your feelings and to distinguish some areas of your life which need a fresh commitment.

The Power of Positive Doing

You are incredibly important. Look back at RULE NUMBER ONE again. There are an unusual number of personal pronouns. You see, the burden rests upon you. You must recognize that you *are* important.

How significant are you? Think, for just one minute, how extraordinarily complex and wonderful you are. Your mind, body and spirit form a magnificent organism — one which is capable of achieving almost unbelievable feats.

Your body's entire structure, from head to foot, is a miracle of precision engineering and production. No matter which portion of your human "machine" is considered, you should understand what a marvelous mechanism each member is.

Your major organs alone — all 10 of them — perform such unique feats of electric conduction that it takes volumes to explain each one adequately.

If you are an adult of average weight, this is part of what your body accomplishes every day:

- Your heart beats 103,689 times.

- Your blood travels 168,000,000 miles.

- You breathe 23,040 times.

- You inhale 438 cubic feet of air.

- You eat 3 1/4 pounds of food.

- You drink 2.9 quarts of liquids.

- You speak 25,800 to 30,000 words.

- You move specific muscles 750 times.

- Your nails grow .000046 of an inch.

- Your hair grows .01714 of an inch.

- You exercise 7,000,000 brain cells.

A few years ago a group of selected scientists were asked what it would take to construct a computer that could perform all the functions of the human brain. After grueling research, they placed the fundamental information about the brain in a computer, and after many days of theorizing, these specialists concluded that to reproduce the actions and components of a human brain, they would need to build a structure the size of the United Nations Building in New York City and fill it with the latest technology. This massive, complex machinery would require a cooling system with an output equal to Niagara Falls and a power source that would produce as much electricity as is used by the entire state of California!

Even though you may consciously forget more than 90% of what you learn during your lifetime, your brain will store 10 times more information than in the 20 million volumes within the Library of Congress.

There are at least several trillion hard-working cells inside you, some so small that it takes 250 of them placed side-by-side to equal the diameter of the period at the end of this sentence.

How can you think that you are not important?

No single scientific instrument has been developed yet that is as sensitive to the light as is your eye. In the dark, its sensitivity increases 100,000 times so that your naked eye is able to see a faint glow which is less than a thousandth the brightness of a candle's flame, yet it can see the light from stars, the nearest of which is 25 billion miles away!

Your ears are as much acoustic marvels as your eyes are optic phenomenons. The inner ear can detect 15,000 different tones. Not only do these ears perform hearing, they control equilibrium as well.

Your heart beats an average of 75 times a minute, 40 million times a year: that's nearly three billion times in a lifetime. At each beat, the average adult heart discharges about four ounces of blood, nearly 3000 gallons a day, and 650,000 gallons a year: enough to fill more than 81 gasoline tank trucks! Your heart does enough work in one hour to lift an average-sized man to the top of a three-story building, creates enough energy in 12 hours to lift a 65-ton tank car one foot off the ground and generates enough power in a lifetime to lift the largest battleship completely out of the water.

What an amazing person you are, whether you realize it or not. *You are important.* You have value — accept that fact!

Realizing your importance requires a major life-adjustment. If you enjoy being a victim, you may not want to change the cycle. If you are constantly being mistreated, you are cooperating with the treatment. You can begin getting control of your life by putting RULE NUMBER ONE to use in your life.

Can you imagine how much stress and worry would be removed from your life if you only realized how important you are? Worry comes from the belief that you are powerless. You are not powerless. Granted, you are only one of five billion people living on this globe, but there is a reason for you being here. You have more than enough natural intelligence and ability within you to reach any goal you want to achieve.

You are important! Say the words outloud:

I AM IMPORTANT.

Now, begin to believe those words.

Respect Others

Likewise, others are important. This concept is easy to understand, but it is also easily forgotten in the swirl of corporate ventures and personal activities.

As a member of the human race who must interact with others on a personal level every day, you have too much at stake to neglect treating others as equally important.

Something uncanny happens when you begin recognizing that others have great value and are significant. Throughout history, the people and nations who have been truly successful are those who have discovered this fact.

Believing that others are important is a principle which goes much deeper than a constitution or doctrine. It means accepting people as they are, without reservation.

Acknowledging others as important is a choice that you must continually make. Not too many people want to be equally important. But it doesn't matter what others feel about themselves — good or bad — as long as you choose to give them their importance.

Too much assertiveness and management training seems to teach, "I am important, and to heck with everyone else." On the other hand, a lot of people say, "I know everyone else is important and it doesn't matter about me — I will be a victim and martyr." Neither attitude offers long-term productivity.

Giving others importance is not always easy. Offer some people a compliment, and they explain it away or reject it. Too many humans believe they are *not* important — this is the breeding ground for tragedies and injustice.

You can make a difference. Choose to place importance upon others. Whether they accept your gift is immaterial to you. Offering importance is the springboard to long-term success.

Rule Number One
Requires A Firm Commitment

"Believing that you are important and so is everyone else puts you in control of your life," says Jonathan Block, the real estate sales manager who was mentioned in Chapter One. "It gives you control and confidence because you begin realizing that no one can bother you or attack you without your permission. That liberates you to plunge enthusiastically into even the most difficult situations. Believe me, in real estate, a business of numbers, ups-and-downs and trust, RULE NUMBER ONE can mean the difference between success and burnout."

RULE NUMBER ONE, as Jonathan relates, is not a Pollyanna-ish, trite phrase. It is a razor-sharp tool that can surgically transform your life.

One warning: RULE NUMBER ONE must come from the inside. You must feed yourself RULE NUMBER ONE before you can begin giving its benefits to others. That requires a commitment.

I am not talking about some paste-on, pious cloak that you drape over yourself, that you show to the world. It cannot be a phony mask. It must be something that comes from the inside. Others will know the difference.

The most amazing thing is that once you begin to believe and act on RULE NUMBER ONE, others will stop trying to put you down.

But I don't ask you to believe me without question. Put it to use. No one beside you needs to know. Soon, however, you won't be able to hide it!

A Practical Principle

How do I know that RULE NUMBER ONE works? I have lived part of my life without following it, and I have lived part of my life putting it to use. I know the difference, and I choose to practice RULE NUMBER ONE.

I have been presented with plenty of reasons to think that I was not important. I came into the world at an interesting time in history — 5 a.m. on October 25, 1929 — the day after "Black Thursday," the official beginning of the Great Depression. The next decade proved to be the making or breaking of millions of people. Times such as those bring out the best and worst in everyone, and I experienced plenty of both. I discovered the razor-edge of prejudice as a child and grew up as an outsider in an ethnically divided Brooklyn neighborhood. I was a poor student, but no one knew that I was dyslexic. During third grade, I had mastoid problems which financially wiped out my family. I flunked my senior year in high school, yet within a year, I headed a manufacturing department at a large company. I spent the next two decades on a roller coaster trying to discover the meaning of success. By that time I had accomplished many top-level achievements in the field of industrial and aerospace engineering.

Along the way, RULE NUMBER ONE helped me change my direction from feeling like a hurt, helpless victim to becoming a purposeful, prosperous person.

I know that RULE NUMBER ONE works — personally and professionally. I have seen it transform tense workplace situations into team-oriented hotbeds. Put this precision-like tool to use in your life.

Time For Yourself

What kind of person do you want to be? Do you want to live the remainder of your life out of control, or do you want to begin putting your life into proper priority?

Accept the challenge I have issued to thousands of people at my seminars and during consulting sessions. Begin saying RULE NUMBER ONE at least three times a day — *out loud*. You don't have to wake up the entire neighborhood, but just say the words loud enough for your own ears to hear:

**I AM IMPORTANT; SO IS EVERYONE
ELSE.**

**I WILL NEVER USE MY IMPORTANCE TO
PUT ANYONE DOWN.**

**I WILL NEVER — NEVER — *NEVER*
ALLOW ANYONE TO USE THEIR
IMPORTANCE TO PUT ME DOWN.**

I suggest that you quote RULE NUMBER ONE *out-loud* when you get up, at least once during midday and before you retire. When possible, say it as you look at yourself in a mirror. By the end of the first week, you will have reinforced this principle at least 21 times. That's more than 84 positive affirmations by the end of the next month. You have everything to gain!

Says Douglas Van Dyke, a welding company owner from New Hampshire:

"I have observed that changes from incorporating RULE NUMBER ONE and the other YES Course homework are much more visible to others than they are to the person doing the work. If you ask a person if he or she has changed, the answer will most likely be, 'Not too much.' But others will probably notice significant changes. The people in my company who have done the homework have become more open, more positive, more in control. As time has gone by, the changes become evident even to themselves."

Do you have one minute a day to begin changing your life? Of course you do. That is only 20 seconds, three times a day, if you talk slowly. But will you consider yourself important enough to prioritize this time for yourself?

I can say from experience that many, many people have used this tool to revolutionize their lives, businesses and careers. You can, too!

A Final Note

What would happen if you really felt important? How would this inner knowledge change the way you handle situations in the marketplace or at home?

Could others put you down? They could not if your strength came from an inward resource, rather than outward circumstances, for their words would not matter. Therefore, you would not be allowing others to use their importance to put you down.

Would you have to put anybody else down if you felt that you were important? Of course not!

Use this precise, practical tool. Learning means DO-ING. Feed yourself RULE NUMBER ONE outloud at least three times a day. You will begin feeling more positive about yourself. This fuels your importance. That action becomes self-propelling, then creates a vital, positive cycle.

Other people will see the change. You will see that others like to be around men, women and children who feel good about themselves. The more you observe RULE NUMBER ONE, the more you will attract people around you who also want to observe this life-changing principle.

Positive +++♥++ Steps

(1) Put RULE NUMBER ONE to work in your life.

(2) You are an incredible machine, computer and structure — you are important.

(3) Something uncanny happens when you begin recognizing the fact that others have great value, are significant and should be treated as important.

(4) RULE NUMBER ONE is practical, both personally and professionally.

Rule Number Two 4
—Absolute Honesty

I'll be what I want to be;
I'll do what I want to do.
I'll not step on others to get there, you see,
Because they're as important as me and you.

I'll forgive them and they'll forgive me;
My mind will be filled with good thoughts.
Whatever will be will be,
And a pessimist I certainly am not.

I am what I allow in my mind,
So when I get mad I'll soon be glad;
And when I give to others I will find
Someone will return that goodness I had.

I'll listen to myself and will know
That my success in life depends on me.
I'll make a friend instead of a foe,
As love is really the key.
I must save time for myself, too,
And be honest with one and all;
For without me what would I do?
I know I never will fall.

—KATHY HUDDLESTON
YES Graduate

Self-Delusion

America's only emperor lived in San Francisco in the last century and was mildly mad. Noblest and best known of all early California characters, Joshua A. Norton was a successful businessman when speculation in the rice market brought financial ruin. Whether this clouded his mind or he started it as a joke, he began telling everyone he was "Emperor of these United States."

This thought grew into an obsession, until in a 1853 printed proclamation he officially claimed himself to be emperor by an act of the California legislature. He strutted the streets in a colorful costume, complete with a sword and plume.

Citizens of San Francisco were amused by the harmless ploy and went along with the self-styled emperor. They gave him recognition through free tickets to opening night events, with newspaper publicity and by permitting him to collect small taxes while issuing his own currency. It was all done in fun, and the emperor became a fixture in the city for several years.

However, all of this was very serious to him and he believed in his position. When tension developed in Mexico, he expanded his authority to "emperor of these United States and Protector of Mexico." When the tragic figure—object of many practical jokes—died in 1880, he had 10,000 curious citizens at his funeral. He had lived and died in his own delusions.

"What a futile sham," we scoff. Is it so unusual? Although most people are not so self-deluded as to believe that they are royalty, many of us are chronically dishonest with ourselves and others.

This dishonesty goes deeper than you may think, much deeper.

Are You Judgemental
Or Non-Judgemental?

I would like you now to take a very solemn, personal pledge. If you are left-handed, hold up your left hand. If right-handed, raise your right hand. And I would like you to repeat this pledge:

I PLEDGE TO BE NON-JUDGEMENTAL OF MYSELF OR ANYONE ELSE . . . EVER!

Please write that pledge in your notebook. Write it big, because the sentence can change your life as you tap into The Power of Positive Doing. The easy part is writing it, the hard part is doing it.

Why is it hard? Why are we judgemental?

Suppose that you discover your behavior is sometimes like that of a spoiled four-year-old. What is the tendency when you discover these things?

Often we put ourselves down. Or we ignore it. We may say, "I'm not as bad as that . . . I'm not as bad as my boss or Sally or Jimmy."

We tend to either hide from it or put ourselves down, don't we?

Why? Why is it hard to be non-judgemental?

One word: programming. Our society has taught most of us well. How can we not be judgemental? Everything about our way of life is based on comparisons and situations.

We have been trained to always be judgemental. From the earliest ages, we are encouraged to compare people:

"You sure look like your daddy."

"Why don't you act more like Johnny?"

"You only got one 'A' on your report card?"

We grow up wanting to be with the *in*-crowd. We want to have a *best* friend. We want to obtain the newest car. In the corporate world, we look longingly at the person who gets the corner office, has access to top executives or receives exclusive perks.

Those who don't desire our goals or match our personal ideals are judged accordingly. As a result, our lives always seem to involve some form of judging.

If you are looking at the other person's success, what are you doing about your own? If you are like a large majority of people, you may be so busy viewing someone else's success that you have little time to empower yourself.

Being non-judgemental means accepting yourself. Totally!

If you are looking at someone else as a success, and looking at yourself as a non-success — you are being judgemental.

It is fine to look at other people, but don't judge. What happens is that we tend to look at someone who seems so much better or worse than we are. We look at them so judgementally. We don't say, well, that person has made a million dollars (that is perhaps a fact), but we tend to say, he is great—he has done wonderful things. (We color the facts.)

He could have even done it dishonestly, and he might not have all the happiness or all the success that we think, but we tend to be judgemental. Being factual is not judgemental, but comparisons or generalizations are.

Here is the basic way to sort out whether you are being judgemental (usually harmful) or making judgements (often constructive):

- A judgement is based on fact.

- Being judgemental is always based on emotion or past programming/prejudice.

There are lots of ways that we are judgemental. We compare ourselves. We label. Many people are so judgemental of themselves that they have to use their titles or their professions as labels.

If someone were to ask you what you do and you say, I'm a nurse. That's a fact.

But if you are using that as a label, then it becomes judgemental.

When you are in a group, listen to how many people label themselves. During the first session of YES classes, I often hear a woman say, "I am Jane Q. Jones, and I am the mother of five children." Or, "Hi, I'm John Q. Jones, an internist at General Hospital."

Having five children or being an internist may be a fact, but when you introduce yourself as the mother of five children, you have already created a label for yourself. You have created a box.

So it is the way you say it. You can say, I am so and so, and I have five children. Or you can say I am the mother of five children. That might be judgemental, depending upon how you say it and the words you use.

Why Is It Important To Be Non-Judgmental?

We have always been very judgemental, but I am asking you to spend some time being non-judgemental.

Why do you think it might be important? Here are three reasons:

(1) Being non-judgemental helps you deal strictly with the facts.

   In today's climate, dealing with the facts is somewhat difficult. The media doesn't help, since "the Fourth Branch of Government" increasingly promotes a reporter or journalist's interpretation of the facts. Headlines and lead-in paragraphs form as much as 65% of the public's entire concept of news events.

   In fact, when you think about it, people often overhear a word or two, and they develop an entire scenario about what's going on, and years later they will repeat to you the story — you say, "Where on earth did they ever get that idea?" They were judgemental about what happened. They were also absolutely certain about what happened.

(2) Being non-judgemental helps you enjoy clearer communications when dealing with events, yourself and other people. It helps you to avoid misperceptions.

(3) Better relationships is another benefit of becoming less judgemental. One of the

greatest problems between loved ones is the mis-understanding caused by misinterpretations and judging patterns.

Presuming what is in someone else's mind also is judgemental.

The secret to being less judgemental rests in the learned ability to accept another person — all people — as they are, not what you want them to be.

Being non-judgemental is not just a good business practice; it is essential to living functionally in today's world.

But how do you become less judgemental?

Throughout The Power of Positive Doing, there are two and only two major guidelines to help you through each of the 12 strategies and the rest of your life. You have already learned RULE NUMBER ONE in Chapter Three:

I AM IMPORTANT; SO IS EVERYONE ELSE.

I WILL NEVER USE MY IMPORTANCE TO PUT ANYONE DOWN.

I WILL NEVER — NEVER — *NEVER* ALLOW ANYONE TO USE THEIR IMPORTANCE TO PUT ME DOWN.

That is the start. Here is the second central principle.

Rule Number Two

The second rule builds upon the idea of being non-judgemental. It deals with personal and professional integrity. Read these words outloud and begin programming yourself with them at least three times a day:

I AM NON-JUDGEMENTAL AND ABSOLUTELY HONEST WITH MYSELF AND OTHERS — ALWAYS.

This is as basic as a person can get. The corporate implications of the need for honesty are highly publicized. In virtually every major survey of desirable leadership characteristics, top executives, middle managers and supervisors and nonmanagerial workers invariably place one characteristic at the top of the list: **honesty** (to be held in respect, free from deceit).

James Kouzes and Barry Posner, in conjunction with professor Warren Schmidt, the American Management Association and the Federal Executive Institute Alumni Association, surveyed thousands of workers, asking them what they considered to be the most important leadership traits. The majority, 83% to be exact, expressed belief that a person must be *honest* before workers are willing to grant that individual the title "leader".[1]

That's what workers say about their superiors. What about the view from above?

Learning Systems of Stamford, Connecticut, polled a number of the nation's leading senior executives, asking them to identify and rank the personal qualities they

---

1. James M. Kouzes and Barry Z. Posner, *The Leadership Challenge* (San Francisco: Jossey-Bass, 1987), pp. 16-17.

hope to find in a successor. *Honesty* ranked first on the list.[2]

Yet according to a recent *New York Times*/CBS poll of workers, only 32% of the public believes that most corporate executives are honest. Conversely, 55% think that most are not honest! There is clearly a gap between what we admire and what the public thinks it is getting.

The rewards for being honest are immeasurable, not just the immediate benefits, but in terms of sustained success and long-range productivity.

---

2. *Working Smart* (Stamford, CT: Learning Systems, 1987).

Positive Doing Insights

HONESTY

Quickly jot ideas into your notebook. Ask yourself:

(1) Is it okay to lie about your age?

(2) When you get mad at friends, do you think of ways to get revenge?

(3) Have you exaggerated your work experience on a job application?

(4) Is lying about your weight normal?

(5) Is exceeding the speed limit dishonest?

(6) Does being truthful put an individual at a distinct disadvantage?

(7) Is it dishonest to make personal phone calls on the job?

(8) Is distorting the truth okay as long as it doesn't hurt anybody?

What do your answers say about you? Are you pleased with how honest you are with yourself and others? Is this an area that seems helpful or hurtful to your personal and professional development?

What Is Absolute Honesty?

Honesty, in its deepest sense, relates to the way you talk with yourself and other people. The sad fact is that all of us lie a lot. We are especially good at being dishonest with ourselves.

For instance, if you say, "I'll *try* to get there," what you really mean is, "I am not making it a top priority. In fact, I may not get there at all."

Is it lying to say, "I'll try?" It is if you don't plan on going. If you don't want to be somewhere at a certain time, something will almost always happen to delay or keep you from coming.

We create the things we want. Since we don't want to take responsibility or make clear-cut choices, we tend to use excuses. We say, "I'll try," when we really want to say, "I don't want to go."

We don't communicate clearly to ourselves, so we don't communicate to others. Later we will say, "Well, if my car hadn't broken down, or if it hadn't rained — I would have been there."

If I really wanted to go some place, then I would have made sure that my car was in good running order by taking it and getting it fixed. If there was a snowstorm, then I would have started out early enough.

If something happens to prevent your appearance, you call up and say, "I'm not coming."

But you don't TRY. That is unclear communication. It is dishonesty — though often at a subconscious level. And when we are not clear with our communication, then we tend to be untruthful or to lie. We just don't call it lying, because that is one of life's negative words.

Self-Sabotage

Dishonesty comes in many forms. Anytime I talk about subconscious dishonesty, I am always reminded about the woman who came to her first YES session. It was a Thursday, and the day before she had just become a grandmother.

Her daughter — the new mother — was somewhat overweight, but only when she went to the doctor for "stomach pains," did she discover that she was pregnant, very pregnant. Two days later she and her husband were the proud parents of a whopping 8.5 pound boy.

She was asked one week before the birth, "Are you expecting?" and she replied, "Absolutely not!" But the reality remained that she was nine months pregnant. Her intentions were honorable, since she didn't believe she was with child. But, according to the true facts she was lying. She did have a baby inside her. Undoubtedly there had been a number of signals, but she had not discovered the truth that was growing inside her. She learned, as novelist Aldrous Huxley said, "Facts do not cease to exist because they are ignored."

You see, absolute honesty deals with the facts. Half a fact is a whole falsehood. If it is not a fact, then it is a lie. This has nothing to do with a person's standards or morality. Call it a non-fact if you dislike the word "lie."

People throughout history have thrived on "true" falsehoods. Lives have been lost because "truth" was actually a lie. Until 1492, nearly all the world's finest intellectuals believed the earth to be flat, and in England, a "Flat Earth Society" (seriously!) still exists. Until the last century, "bleeding" bad blood from ill patients was an acceptable practice among physicians; George Washington died as a result of "bleeding."

Both "facts" were not true. Either it is one or the other. Either you are dead or alive. Think of things like that. You can be one or the other, not wandering around in the gray area.

Bob Wentworth, a New England businessman, remembers how difficult that was:

> "The entire concept of ABSOLUTE HONESTY was quite a shock at first. I thought it was a nice idea, but I wondered what in the world it had to do with professional development. After accepting the idea, with admitted difficulty, I quickly began to see that I no longer had to worry about what I said in any situation. Everyone involved is better off. The people I talk to have a better opportunity to see who I am, and they don't have to keep guessing where I am coming from. This attitude on my part has helped build confidence among the people who work with me. They know I don't play games — that I won't duck a confrontation, but I am also willing to hear and understand what they say."

You must be specific and factual to avoid unclear communications and being judgemental. Absolute honesty helps you avoid the situation spoken 200 years before Christ by Petronius:

> "We tend to meet any new situation by reorganizing, and a wonderful method it can be for creating the illusion of progress while producing confusion, inefficiency, and demoralization."

Instead of reorganizing your beliefs concerning honesty and integrity, why not peer inside yourself and see how telling the truth, especially to yourself, can make all the difference in the world?

The Power of Positive Doing   67

Self-Inspection

Think of ways that you are not factual. Have you ever set yourself a goal, perhaps losing 10 pounds, but instead of losing 10, you gain two. Was losing 10 really a goal? No! According to the facts, you were kidding yourself — lying to yourself.

Most people tend to set goals, then put subconscious blocks in the way. I know lots of people who say they want to be successful, lose weight, stop smoking, be a better lover or exercise more, but there is always something that comes up to keep them from reaching their goals. It all boils down to a question of honesty!

People say:

"I really would have been on time IF ONLY . . ."

"Everything would have been different IF . . ."

"I wanted to do it, BUT . . ."

You and I keep lying to ourselves. Intentions don't matter. What matters are the facts.

Oh, perhaps you and I can justify everything by saying that we don't usually tell "out and out" lies — the ones where we can get caught. But we create lies, not just by our *words*, but by our *thoughts* and *actions*. Sometimes we lie within all three of these areas at once.

When I say one thing and act another way — at home, on the job or on vacation where no one knows who I am — I am lying. I am also creating confusion, not only for myself, but for those around me who are trying to communicate with me.

If you, for example, tell a loved one or a superior, "I will be back by 2 o'clock," but don't arrive back until 3 o'clock, you cause harm with your falsehood, well-intentioned or not.

Worse yet, as with the not-pregnant/very pregnant young woman, we lie when we don't even know we are lying. Those are the most harmful lies, for we are lying to ourselves. And, despite an adage to the contrary, the things you don't know CAN hurt you.

Why don't we want to change? Usually we have a vested interest in maintaining our lies. Think of history's "truths" which had to be changed — the flat world, germs, automobiles, flight — people had to face a major reorganization when their lies were exposed and a better way offered.

It is perfectly normal for you and me to want to avoid looking inside, to seek to uncover the ways that we lie.

Difficulty In Changing

I don't want you to finish this chapter, close the book and say, "Okay, I need to be absolutely honest with myself and others, so I will never lie again." That isn't possible. If you have been lying in certain ways all your life, all I want you to do is take a look inside yourself. Catch yourself when you lie — to yourself and others — and force yourself to say, "That's really not the truth, so obviously I am lying."

Just spend time examining what you have been doing and how you think.

You don't have to lie, not even with those so-called "white lies."

Don't change anything right now, just look at the way you think. Become more aware of how your mind works. You will have plenty of opportunities to make positive changes as you read further.

A Final Note

Who are you? Whether you are a CEO, a clerical worker or a truck driver, undoubtedly you are a composite of several different persons:

(1) The person other people think you are.

(2) The person you think other people think you are.

(3) The person you want other people to think you are.

(4) The person you really are, when no one else is looking and when there is little chance of being found out, no matter what you do.

Until you can merge those four YOUs into one YOU, you continue to relegate yourself to a life without peace and with limited positive influence.

Never forget this fact: believing in things does not make them so. If you don't know you are lying, then you are going to continue to act as if those facts were true. That keeps perpetuating your false ideas.

Likewise, the more honesty you develop, the more clearly you can see deep into your self.

Positive +++♥++ Steps

(1) Self-dishonesty goes deeper than you may think, much deeper. We have been trained to always be judgemental.

(2) Make a pledge to be non-judgemental of yourself or anyone else . . .ever!

(3) Live by RULE NUMBER TWO: "I am non-judgemental and absolutely honest with myself and others — always.

(4) Honesty, in its deepest sense, relates to the way you talk with yourself and other people.

Negative Support 5

Information

A journey down roads less traveled
 The roads less traveled by my mind
A new way to look at myself and my world
Re-visiting a familiar place but approaching from a new
 road
"Re-thinking" an experience and "re-storing" it in a new
 way
Dare to take the road less traveled in thought and
 in action
There are many possible roads
The roads I take and the roads I make reflect who I am
Yes, many roads, but only two kinds of people
Those going somewhere and those going nowhere
Those doing what they want to do and those doing what
 others want them to do
Choose to take control of your life
Make your own choices, with a new awareness
These words of Robert Frost are one of my favorite lines
 of verse:
  "I took the road less traveled and that has made all
  the difference."

—GORDON HUDDLESTON
YES Graduate

The Ham

Joe and Judy, a newly married couple, were still in the throes of marital bliss on Sunday as they came home from their honeymoon cruise. Since both planned to return to work on Monday, and being very equal-minded and self-sufficient, the happy couple decided to alternate nights for preparing the dinner.

On Monday, Joe, a city boy, cooked his mother's recipe for spaghetti, and it was a delicious hit. On Tuesday, Judy, a down-home gal, decided to bake a daisy ham. Joe watched with a quizzical look as she took the ham from the container, cut an inch or two from both ends, then placed it in a pan to cook.

"I'm just wondering," Joe said, "why did you cut the ends off the ham?"

"That's how you make daisy ham," Judy muttered matter-of-factly. "Everybody knows that's how you do it."

"Not everybody," Joe posed delicately. "My mom never does that to her hams."

"Well, I can't help that!" Judy retorted sharply. "You always cut off both ends. That's the way it's done."

"Where did you learn that?" Joe asked sharply.

"My mother," she replied.

"Where did she learn it?" he inquired.

"Ask her yourself!"

"Okay," Joe accepted the challenge, dialing the telephone.

Within seconds, Judy's mother had repeated the same lines as her daughter. "Everyone cuts the ends off a daisy ham. I learned it that way from my mother, and she learned it from my grandmother."

Several telephone calls later, Joe tenaciously dialed the number of a nearby age-care center where Judy's great-grandmother lived.

"Where did you learn to cut off both ends before baking a daisy ham?" Joe asked her, motioning Judy to listen on an extension phone.

"Well," the octogenarian began, "when my husband, God rest his soul, and I immigrated from the old country, we were newlyweds just like you two lovebirds, and I didn't have but one small baking pot. I always had to lop off a little bit from both ends of a daisy ham so that I could put it in the pan! I guess my kids learned that way, because we used that same pan for years."

Joe couldn't resist asking, "But why does your daughter and her daughter and all the rest of your family still make daisy hams that way — even though they use larger pans?"

Said Judy's great-grandmother with a laugh, "To tell you the truth, I've been wondering about that one, myself, all these years!"

Products Of The Past

The "daisy ham" story, though updated, is based on a true account.

"How silly," you say. I don't think so. I never cease to be amazed at the "daisy ham" narratives I hear from the people I meet, either in corporate or seminar settings.

Here are a few common stories:

- Families continue specific Christmas or Hanukkah traditions, though no one remembers why.

- People buy a brand of automobile, clothing, laundry soap — just because "our family has always bought that kind."

- Men and women continue working in professions, wishing they would have chosen a different vocation, but puppeting the line, "I just knew that it would make my parents very happy for me to be a doctor," or "I couldn't decide what I wanted to be, and this sales job came up at a time when I needed it, so . . ."

How many personal "daisy ham" stories could you share about yourself?

I call these screens or filters by an easy-to-remember name: NEGATIVE SUPPORTIVE INFORMATION, or NSIs, for short. What do I mean?

All of us are products of our pasts. Our disciplines, education, training, experiences and traditions help form who we are. None of these components are necessarily bad or good, but they can become destructive unless we examine each to see if they are fact or falsehood.

NEGATIVE PATTERNS

In your notebook on two opposing pages, using an entire page for each activity, do the following:

(1) On the left-hand page, take one minute or less to draw a picture of yourself.

(2) On the right-hand page, take one minute or less to sketch a picture of your world.

FOR YOUR MAXIMUM BENEFIT, PLEASE DO NOT READ ANY FURTHER UNTIL YOU HAVE COMPLETED QUESTIONS 1 AND 2 ABOVE.

There are no right or wrong answers, but let me share a few clues for consideration, based on interviews I have conducted with thousands of people over the past three decades as well as research completed by the former University of Washington professor and imminent psychologist, Dr. Robert C. Burns.

- Examine the size of the pictures, as compared to the full sheet of notebook paper. A *little picture* may mean a little self/little world feeling. A *big picture* often reveals a big self/big world.

- Compare the size of the self-picture to the sketch of the world. A *little self to big world* probably means that you feel you owe the world something or that the world has power and control over you. A *big self to a little world* tends to point toward feelings that you have power over the world or that you feel the world owes you something. When both are relatively the *same-size*, it probably reveals a life in balance.

- On your self-picture, *large ears* suggest sensitivity to criticism.

- Drawing an unusually *large head* suggests high intellectual aspirations, while a *small head* suggests feelings of social or intellectual inadequacy.

- Unusually *large eyes* may infer suspicion or hypersensitivity, while *small ones* suggest introspection or the wish not to see.

- *Short arms* suggest lack of power or ambition.

- *Missing feet* suggest instability or a lack of roots. People who tend to run away from life-situations almost always draw themselves without feet or lower extremities.

- A *big nose* shows an exploding anger. *No nose* indicates a suppressed anger.

- A *long neck* suggests a dependent personality, while a *short neck* implies bull-necked independence.

These are interpretations, but they are hardly engraved-in-stone rules. Use them only to look deeper as you seek to unlock The Power of Positive Doing inside yourself.

Elephant Stakes

Throughout the world, the pattern remained relatively unchanged until recently. When a circus came to town, the handlers would first take the elephants off the train or wagons. These two-ton pachyderms would be hitched to wagons, which were packed with mounds of materials to take to the fairgrounds or coliseum. After the traditional "elephant parade," the workers began putting up thousands of pounds of huge poles, tents and the spider-web network of ropes and equipment. The elephants did this work all day long, getting ready for the circus.

The amazing part is this: at the end of the day, keepers would march the elephants out in the back field and take a small rope — roughly a tenth of the size of the huge tent ropes — and tie it around the animal's ankles, then fasten it to a small metal stake in the ground. The elephants stayed there all night because they knew, absolutely knew, that they could not get loose.

They believed the little stake was holding them down because, as newborn elephants, they had been trained that way.

Do you have stakes which hold you down? If you do, that's your NEGATIVE SUPPORTIVE INFORMATION.

As a child, you were probably told, "Don't talk to strangers." It was a simple, straightforward statement, offered with good intentions to keep you from being hurt or kidnapped, but it is no longer valid in your life. If you haven't learned to talk to strangers by now, you are still living with your parents or are holed up some where as a hermit.

NSIs come in lots of packages. You may have been told, "You are too little to do that." Today you may hear, "You are too big to act like that." How do you know if those statements are true or false unless you examine them?

"Luck" NSIs are often harmful, though offered with the best of intentions. "Tough luck," someone mutters. "Good luck," another salutes. Or, "Boy, doesn't he seem to be having a lot of bad luck lately?" Luck ignores reality. Reality is based on the fact that you are a product of your choices. If you are serious about taking responsibility for your life, you must reach the point where you realize that you are what you are because of what you have allowed through your mind in the past. If that is true — which, of course, it is — then tomorrow you will be whatever you choose to be because of what you allow to pass through your mind from this point.

Do you want control of your life or not? Admittedly, it is frightening to take control. It infers that you can no longer place blame on yourself or others — it means that you, alone, must take responsibility for your life and your actions.

Don't let "elephant stakes" hold you back anymore! Realize that NSI comes from many places:

- Programming.

- Parents.

- Teachers.

- Ministers, rabbis or other religious instructors.

- Police.

- Elected officials.

- Advertising.

- The media.

- Celebrities.

NSIs are not bad or good, wrong or right. NSIs may have been good for you during a specific period of development.

Regardless, they are still there. Your parents and other authority figures were doing the best they knew, just as the elephant trainers were just doing a job when they trained the small pachyderms to stay in one place; however, the adult elephants were still limited by those small ropes and stakes.

But if you allow yourself to be limited by your own "elephant stakes," how do you know if they are helpful or harmful unless you identify and examine them? Undoubtedly you have within you a number of screens that keep you from seeing what is real and truthful — perhaps they are illusions, or maybe they are in the form of emotional baggage. Understand this: anything that holds you back from growth is negative and retardant. If something or some form of instruction renders you powerless, it is up to you to rip up those "elephant stakes."

Personal NSIs

You can learn to recognize your NSIs. Listen to yourself. Question your patterns. Ask yourself, "Why do I do _____ that way?"

Earlier you sketched a picture of yourself. Unfortunately, it is not quite as easy to draw a comprehensive schematic of your inner self. The best way to begin unraveling your NSIs is to detect patterns in your speech and thoughts.

On whom do you place blame when something happens? In moments of crisis, what thoughts arise? When you are being absolutely silent, with no interference, what flashes in your mind?

Begin writing down patterns of speech and thought in your notebook. You may start to see how controlled you are by NSIs.

Unlearning NSIs

An impeccably-dressed salesperson from the city was driving down a rural road, intent on reaching her destination in time. She wanted to get to Smithville and was making excellent time until she came to an unmarked fork in the road. Not knowing which direction to take, she figured that she should stick with the best paved road, so continued on her way. Eventually the pavement ended, but the gravel road looked fine, so she kept going. After several more miles, the road deteriorated into a rutted dirt path. Gratefully, she approached the outskirts of a little village. She went into a general store, bought a soft-drink and asked one of the local fellows, "What town am I in?"

"Town?" one whiskered chap laughed. "This ain't no town, but what it is, is Jonesville."

"Well," the woman asked, "if this is Jonesville, I must have taken the wrong fork back down the road. I guess the obvious question is how I can cut across to Smithville from where I am right now. Can you tell me how?"

The local man thought for a moment without speaking. He knew the area well, and that if this elegant woman had a 4-wheel drive vehicle, she could probably travel two miles around a rugged mountain road, through a river-bottom valley and come out within a mile of Smithville. "But this woman?" he thought. "Not in her pretty car."

"Woman," he finally muttered, "you can't get there from here."

"What do you mean?" she asked incredulously. "Of course I can get there, even if it means going back to the fork in the road and going from there."

"That'd be the best way," he agreed. "You can get there from the fork, but you can't get there from here."

That is what you must do as you unlearn NSIs. Of course you can get to your destination: "unstaking your personal elephants." But you will probably have to back up and go from a different direction. There are many blocks in your way, but backing up first gives you a better road to travel.

Of course you have been successful in many areas of life up to this point. You have gotten where you are and you know that certain things work for you. So when I present some ideas, you naturally have a tendency to say, "Well, that isn't the way I do it" or "That isn't the way it works for me."

A woman who attended the YES course many years ago related how she was forced to face an NSI. She was a self-taught skier and considered very good in her home area, but she wanted to be a competitive racer. She practiced very hard. She worked at every aspect of her skiing skills. She became very, very good and began placing in the top five finishers of the races she entered. A year later she was still at that same performance level. She just could not get over that "hump" which could mean the top levels of competition.

Undaunted, she went to a leading ski coach and explained her situation. After he watched her ski, he said, "Well, if you want to become the racer that you'd like to be, you will have to *unlearn most of what you know about skiing.*"

At first she felt like exploding, "Are you out of your mind? How in the world could I unlearn something that is working so well? Can't you just fine-tune what I am already doing?"

But the instructor was considered the best, so she decided to do whatever he said. At first her performance dipped miserably. She wondered many times if she was doing the right thing. After months of intensive training, however, her performance level began rising rapidly. Within a year of her first encounter with the celebrated instructor, she won the first of many championship trophies.

Likewise, if you want to improve aspects of your life, it may be needful to unlearn certain things that have perhaps worked "well enough" for you, but not good enough.

As you examine your NSIs and move into the following chapters, I can guarantee that you will not have to unlearn everything — only certain things.

A Final Note

When a person does not understand something, or when it is convenient to ignore reality, that man, woman or child generally ascribes that "unknown" to luck or fate.

What you are today is no accident. Accept that fact, and you are light-years ahead of the majority of human beings.

We live in a cause-and-effect world. You are what you are today because of what you have allowed to go through your mind in the past. Tomorrow you will become whatever you become as a result of what you allow through your mind from this point forward.

The NSIs you have learned are inside your self, so the unlearning has to occur in the same place.

Do you unlearn NSIs overnight? Of course not. How long did it take for you to arrive at this place? Unlearning NSIs is a life-long opportunity to keep improving and "unstaking your elephants."

Unlearning NSIs implies a frightening, bittersweet responsibility, doesn't it? It means that you are in control of everything you do; therefore, you cannot justify blaming anyone — your parents, authority figures, past "accidents," hurts or successes.

The questions must become centered on right now. What do you want in your life? Do you want to be sick? Do you want to have accidents? Do you want to do great things? Do you want to be in control at all times?

The choices belong to you. You can create your own future. In the following chapters, I will continue to unveil more strategies of The Power Of Positive Doing.

What are YOU going to do about unlearning your NSIs and unleashing your future?

Positive ✚✚✚♥✚✚ *Steps*

(1) All of us are products of our past.

(2) Do you have "elephant stakes" or NEGATIVE SUPPORTIVE INFORMATION (NSIs) which hold you down?

(3) How do you know if your NSIs are helpful or harmful unless you identify and examine them?

(4) You can learn to recognize your NSIs. Listen to yourself. Question your thought and speech patterns.

(5) You may have to back up and unlearn your NSIs before going forward.

Goal-Setting 6
Versus Pole-Climbing

The Sun is whispering on my face,
It beckons me to look, to look,
To see the orange beauty in the sunset
and not to think of it as an ending;
The last rays of autumn that close the
    season.

I lost the evening in mourning and tears,
and I can never get it back,
nor do I want it.

There will never again be lost moments,
lost days,
or you.

When the sun comes up behind me
    tomorrow,
I will revel in the glory and passion of
    living,
and then I will see things clearly once
    more.

—ROBERT SZUCS
YES Graduate

Illusions

Britain's Sir Samuel Baker used to tell this true story: Many years ago, when Egyptian troops first conquered Nubia, a regiment was marching through the Nubian desert. The men, being on a limited allowance of water, suffered from extreme thirst. They had seen mirages before, but on one extremely hot afternoon, they spied a beautiful lake and oasis several miles out of the way.

"Take us to that lake," the commander demanded his Arabian guide.

"But it is no lake," insisted the Arab. "I know this area. We must keep moving to the East. We cannot waste precious time by wandering from our course."

In the argument that ensued, the guide refused to budge. Words led to blows, and the Arab was killed by the soldiers, whose lives depended upon his guidance.

Undaunted, the commander and his men headed toward the lush oasis. At length the delusion vanished. The lake turned to burning sand.

One soldier entered these words in his diary, "Raging thirst and horrible despair! The pathless desert and the murdered guide. . .lost! Lost!"

No man left the desert alive. They were subsequently discovered, parched and withered corpses, by a group of Arab guides.

Paradoxes

Life is filled with illusions and mirages. Nearly everyone I have met has a list of disappointing times when they followed a lifestyle, a career, an ideal or a leader, only to discover that the path left them more empty than ever.

One of the most cruel deceptions is the one that allows you to think that you are reaching your goals, while you are actually toiling on a treadmill.

There is a difference between true goals and mechanistic regimens. That difference relates to inner and outer motivations.

Positive Doing Insights

CHOICES

Quickly jot responses to these questions into your notebook:

(1) Name three people whom you admire? What one trait do you admire about each of them?

(2) What are your three strongest points? Weakest points?

(3) What is the most important change or crisis you may expect to face during the next decade?

(4) What is the most important choice you will have to make during the next few months?

(5) What kind of person would you like to become five years from today? Ten years?

(6) Imagine that it is five years from today. You have just passed away. Suppose an obituary writer at a local newspaper is assigned your story. For what events or accomplishments would you like to be remembered? What sort of achievements do you expect to be listed in your obituary?

SCORING: Based upon your answers, are you satisfied with your progress? What do you need to change or do differently to achieve your goals?

Goals

Life's innovators position themselves better by set-ting goals. You can explore how to adopt an innovative lifestyle by learning how to propel yourself toward suc-cess. You can fuel your inner dreams by learning how to set personal goals.

Consider this: Just as the space shuttle burns up near-ly all of its half-million gallons of fuel just to lift its 74-ton cargo mere inches off the launch pad, so your aspi-rations seem painfully slow and unrewarding before taking shape.

With spacecraft, as in life, the most important ex-pense, effort and mental output must take place before anyone sees results.

Here are three points to ponder:

(1) *Everyone* dreams and sets goals, even if they don't follow up on them. How often have you heard peo-ple say, "I just never set goals," or "I don't believe in goals. That way, I am never disappointed if I don't reach them."

Nonsense! Everyone sets goals *every day*: either to turn off the alarm or keep snoozing, either to eat breakfast or to skip that meal, either to go to work or stay home and watch cartoons, either to pay the bills or let the electricity be switched off, either to run two miles or eat two candy bars. You are con-stantly making choices and setting goals, whether you acknowledge that fact or not.

People have just become so accustomed to setting and reaching those everyday goals that they don't recognize what they are doing. IF YOU CAN SET

EVERYDAY GOALS, REST ASSURED THAT
YOU CAN LEARN TO SET LONGER-TERM
GOALS.

(2) Successful people are generally better dreamers
and goal-setters.

I have worked with thousands of people in my
seminars and consulting work, and I can safely say
that the overwhelming majority of truly successful
people got that way by identifying their personal
dreams and goals, and by following orderly paths
to reach those levels.

(3) Defined and pursued goals give direction to your
life. Without these life-directors, you will get dis-
couraged and lack the persistence to keep piercing
walls of resistance.

Internal motivation is crucial. True goals need to
come from inside you. When goals are set through inner inspiration, a feeling of elation accompanies the fulfillment of those dreams.

Poles

There is a difference between GOALS, which come
from inner motivation, and those generated by outside
stimulus POLEs.
Much like other forms of NEGATIVE SUPPORT-
IVE INFORMATION, POLEs (PATTERNS OF LIV-
ING EXTERNALLY) are based on tradition, habit, manipulation or influence.

How many people do you know who live their lives trying to meet someone else's standards?

- The woman who became a doctor because her dad was a doctor.

- The man who decided to accept the call to the ministry because his mother wanted a son who was a minister.

- The young person who studies extreme hours, working obsessively hard to get good grades in school because he or she doesn't want to disappoint parents.

- The wife and mother who dotes on her children and husband so that everyone will see that she is a "good" mother and wife.

- The professional athlete who wishes he or she could retire.

As with other NSIs, none of these reasons or urges are necessarily bad. The authority figures who set external motivations probably had no negative intent, but those outward standards have become POLEs.

They are treadmills. Even if you reach the top of a POLE, your inner self remains unfulfilled. You can con your outer self, but you can't delude your inner self.

Decisions To Make

You must choose between goals and POLEs as you determine your destination and purpose in life. Consider these differences:

	GOALS	POLES
(1)	Doing exactly what you choose to do.	Doing things because of tradition or habit.
(2)	Come from the inner self.	Externally motivated.
(3)	Fulfilling.	Non-fulfilling.
(5)	Leave you feeling elated, even when you fail.	Leave you feeling empty, even when you reach your objective.
(6)	Push you to higher goals.	Compel you to play safe and POLE-perched.
(7)	Build your potential.	Slash your potential.
(8)	Your dreams and plans.	Someone else's dreams and plans.
(9)	Offer long-term perspective.	Let you view only one POLE at a time.

Goals Give Focus To Your Life

Although POLEs are safer and generally offer visible results more quickly, they also stunt your overall development.

Goals, on the other hand, offer long-term incentives. Your aspirations rise and fall on your goals and through your vision of becoming a success. No plan is ever any better than the goals on which it is founded.

To be effective, as you travel mile after mile on life's highway, your goals must be:

(1) Personal — you must be able to be excited about your goals. They must be internally motivated, since external expectations quickly lose luster.

Properly motivated, you can use your goals to process everything else out and to concentrate all your energies and resources in specific directions.

(2) Specific — the more specific your goals, the better your chances of reaching them.

People who set specific goals make things happen; people who don't set goals end up waiting for something to happen. Wishful thinkers sit around wondering what happened!

(3) Achievable — a goal is not some vague pipedream or "pie-in-the-sky" fable. A good goal is one which causes you to stretch all your abilities, but one which you can be reasonably confident of attaining. Only you know the difference between a true goal and a fantasy.

(4) Practical — to have meaning, goals must be broken down into three categories:

- Long-range goals cover several years, but usually not more than 10.

- Intermediate goals are set by breaking long-range goals down into annual, or semi-annual steps, always leading toward the long-range goals you have set.

- Short-range goals come from breaking down your intermediate goals into monthly or weekly steps toward your long-range goals.

Everything you do, especially as you set your goals, has a definite impact on where you are going to be five years from now.

(5) Timed and dated — if you want to start reaching mileposts up the road, give yourself definite deadlines for reaching them, then hold yourself to those deadlines.

(6) Important to you — the key to all discipline is desire; the more you desire something, the easier self-discipline becomes.

For example, it might be hard for you to boost your productivity by 20% during the next year just to prove you can do it or just because your superior says that you should.

But if you plan this 20% boost as a means of achieving a dream (perhaps better investments or buying a new sportscar) you may be surprised to find out what you can do.

However, too many people buy the sportscar on credit, then they are forced to boost their income by 15% to make the payments. That is not self-discipline; that is bondage.

(7) Self-promised — most of us are a lot better at keeping the vows we make to others than we are at keeping the pledges we make to ourselves. Maybe that's why other people always seem to have more confidence in us than we have in ourselves!

Goals only work when you consider them to be promises you have made to yourself, and keep them with the same tenacity with which you would keep a promise to your dearest loved one.

(8) Balanced — your goals should cover every aspect of your life. Many people fail to reap the full benefit of setting goals because they confine them only to their careers.

I never cease to be amazed at how the most outstanding goal-setters among business and civic leaders are sometimes complete failures at setting goals with their families.

Likewise, some college professors have marvelous intellectual goals, yet they completely ignore their needs for physical fitness goals.

A good set of goals covers every area of life:

- Career growth

- Family

- Social development

- Inner well-being

- Financial security

(9) Continuous — your life should be a constantly improving set of stepping stone goals. Goals should enable you to keep expanding your horizons.

What happens if you don't reach your goals? If you gave it your best shot, you will have the deep inner satisfaction of knowing you tried. Like most goal-setters, you will probably double your efforts and keep going.

Even more, you will be miles ahead of where you would have been otherwise. Christopher Columbus determined to open a new trade route to India, but he missed it by thousands of miles. Instead, he discovered the "New World." Numerous cities, a country and even a national holiday commemorate Columbus — not bad for a "failure"!

Look past your barriers and potential failures. Napoleon envisioned Italy, not the Alps. Washington saw victory over the Hessians at Trenton, not the frozen Delaware River. American miler Glenn Cunningham did not concentrate on his burned, scarred legs, but instead visualized himself as an Olympic medalist. George Bush saw past his initial primary defeats, and pointed toward the Presidency.

The majority of men and women see the obstacles, but successful people are able to see past barriers and to view the objectives. That's why POLEs are easier to live with — when you meet someone else's standards, you can always blame them when you feel unfulfilled and dissatisfied.

Goals are risky. You are putting yourself on the proverbial line. If you fail or if you succeed, everything depends upon you. Not many people want to accept that measure of responsibility.

How about you? What will it take to stop you? Your life will never be any more successful than your goals. Become a champion goal-setter, not a frustrated POLE-sitter.

A Final Note

If you have lived as a POLE-sitter, take heart. POLEs can be turned into Goals. In fact, the POLEs set by other people can be turned into milesposts to fuel your motion.

You can choose for yourself. You don't have to feel trapped for the rest of your life. You don't have to spend your days blaming someone.

Set aside a definite time during the next few days to formulate a complete set of goals for every area of your life. Start with long-range goals, then break them down into intermediate and short-range goals.

Life's innovators set goals for themselves and live their lives by those goals. Remember, the poorest person is not the one who has no money, but he or she who lives without dreams and goals. Learn to dream big dreams and set life-changing goals.

You can correct your course! Listen to your inner self. Don't kill your inner guides, or you — as did the Egyptian troops in the desert — will wind up thirsty, despairing and lost.

Positive +++♥++ *Steps*

(1) There is a difference between true goals and mechanistic regimens. That difference relates to inner
and outer motivations.

(2) Life's innovators position themselves better by setting goals generated from within.

(3) POLEs (PATTERNS OF LIVING EXTERNAL-
LY) are based on tradition, habit, manipulation or
influence.

(4) You must choose between goals and POLEs as you
determine your destination and purpose in life.

(5) Become a champion goal-setter, not a frustrated
POLE-sitter.

Go Beyond 7
Positive Thinking By Controlling Your Mind-Switch

I am as steady as stone; as water, true to course,
North Star, my guide.

And I will do what-so-ever I set my heart/my mind to:
Chance everything — risk the dark.

I am a bold adventurer, a pirate of the light.

For it is the hunt — the loving of the game;
The laughter — light, the dance, the bubbling spring
That I am here to be.

Teacher. Lover. True believer.

Now I create myself: again, again, moment by moment.

Hand by wave, foot by slip,
Word by heart thought by truth.

And on and on. Forever — ever once away.

—LUCINDA LAMB
YES Graduate

State Of Mind

I am sure you have noticed by now that my engineering mind, even when I am instructing and consulting in a corporate setting, seems intent on simplifying everything as much as possible.

It is my goal, especially as we move into mental processes, to de-mystify and make less pretentious the entire scope of how our minds work. I am no psychologist, but I have seen my theories work in thousands of lives.

You see, even though you are an integrated person, you are basically composed of two entities:

- Your body

- Your mind

Consider the sketches on the following two pages:

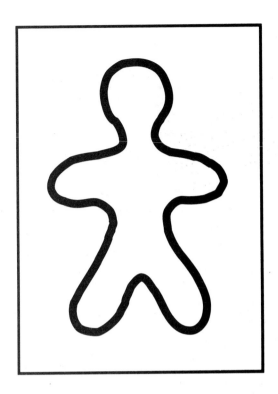

Your body carries out the functions of the mind.

Your mind — some call it the life force or intellect — is not just your brain. It is not merely in your head, but is networked through your entire system.

That mind is actually two spheres. To simplify I will use the letters A and B:

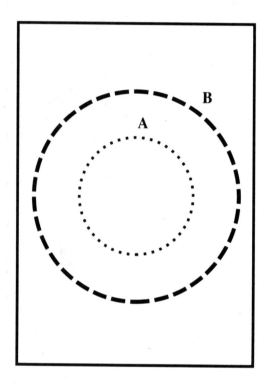

The outer B mind.

The inner A mind.

When you understand how these two aspects of your mind work, THE POWER OF POSITIVE DOING becomes even more of a step-by-step opportunity.

How you use your mind will determine your future as it has already created your present. The idea expressed on page 26 bears repeating at this time:

> *How I think*
> > determines
> What I think
> > determines
> My attitude
> > determines
> What I do
> > determines
> My environment
> > reinforces
> *How I think.*

And the cycle starts all over again, unless YOU CHANGE IT.

How you think is the only thing you can change in that cycle. To shift your mental processes, you must first understand how your mind works in conjunction with your body.

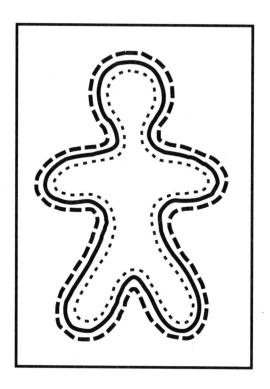

Your body, represented by the solid line, is what everyone sees. Even though you are formed from separate inner and outer components, you are one integrated unit.

Your B mind, represented by the dashed line, deals with the intellect, your conscious. Your B mind deals with the way you structure yourself to deal with the world.

Your A mind, represented by the dotted line, is your great storage area which deals with the emotions, both conscious and unconscious. It is your deepest self, which many people call your self image.

Your B Mind

This outer area of your mental system carries out the outside functions of the mind — the way you dress, walk, comb your hair, act and talk.

When people look at you, they see the results of your B mind. It deals with your intellect and your conscious will. The B mind directs the way you structure yourself to interface with people around you. It is where you *feel* your emotions.

Your A Mind

All that you have experienced is stored inside your A mind. It controls your heartbeat, digestion and involuntary muscles. It is your mental storage, your self-image.

Your A mind controls your emotional progress — the way you view yourself. Inside your body is a series of chemical plants which the A mind controls.

The A mind does not function by accident, but on purpose. What you do, consciously or subconsciously, is always directed by what you store in your A mind.

Yet your A mind is a slave. It will do exactly what it is told to do. It doesn't differentiate between true and false. If you say, "I can never remember names," your A mind knows that every name you have heard is stored inside it, but it will not release the information to your conscious B mind and you cannot remember those names.

Your A mind loves you and would like the best for you, but it will give you whatever you ask. Therefore, you must be careful what you feed A. You must decide what you want to become and feed that information to A. This is simple, but it is not easy.

Your true goals come from your A mind. Inherent within A are goal structures, but since B programs A, B also programs your interpretations of those goals. Quite often, we think we have true goals, but we find that those goals, when reached, don't make us happy because of the wrong programming that we allowed.

For example, have you ever wanted to take time off from your job, but you felt that it would cause problems at work or make your boss unhappy (B mind thoughts)? Probably you went back into your A mind storage and you come out with a thought that said, "I'm not important. Others are more important than I am, so I can't take time off." This was based on programming that you gave A through the years.

But your A mind loves you, and it knows that your body needs time off, so A says, "I'll handle it for you." It then proceeds to send out "sick" signals. A originates thoughts (it controls your inner functions), so despite your B mind, you get sick and have to take time off. This makes you feel out of control.

Your A mind is your greatest resource for goals, peace and truth.

STRIDES TOWARD
UNDERSTANDING YOURSELF

In your notebook write a sentence or two in response to each of the following questions:

(1) What really sets you off?

(2) Does it bother you when you have to deviate from your schedule? Why?

(3) What do you look for in friends?

(4) What bothers you most about relationships which have ended?

(5) Are there any specific events in the past that you haven't been able to forgive or forget?

(6) What terrifies you? Why?

Do you see any patterns or trends? Over the past five years, have you noticed any changes in how you handle emotional snags?

What Is Truth?

Louise Hay, in her nationally bestselling book, *You Can Heal Your Life*, writes:

> "Whatever we believe becomes true for us. If you have a sudden financial disaster, then on some level you may believe you are unworthy of being comfortable with money, or you believe in burdens and debt. Or if you believe that nothing good ever lasts, do you believe that life is out to get you, or, as I hear so often, 'I just can't win.'
>
> "If you seem unable to attract a relationship, you may believe 'Nobody loves me,' or 'I am unlovable.' Perhaps you fear being dominated as your mother was, or maybe you think, 'People just hurt me.'
>
> "If you have poor health, you may believe, 'Illness runs in our family.' Or that you are a victim of the weather. Or perhaps it's, 'I was born to suffer,' or 'It's just one thing after another.'
>
> "Or you may have a different belief. Perhaps you're not even aware of your belief. Most people really aren't. They just see the outer circumstances as being the way the cookie crumbles. Until someone can show you the connection between the outer experiences and the inner thoughts, you remain a victim in life."[1]

You can choose to ignore the networking of your A and B spheres, but check it out before you expel it. The

---

1. Louise Hay, *You Can Heal Your Life* (Santa Monica, CA: Hay House, 1987), pp. 39-40.

next time you want time off, check out your real feelings. Take action.

Anytime I begin feeling ill, I have learned to ask myself questions. Almost always such symptoms as influenza or "colds" reveal feelings of fragmentation or too many things going on at once.

Most of us are not aware of the A inner self or how much effect it has.

This is a irrefutable fact: Whatever the inside world is imagined to be is what the outside world will eventually become.

Control Your Mind Switch

You do not have to live as you now live. You can change not only the way your B mind interprets your world, but you can also change what is stored in your A mind.

If you caused it, why not un-cause it? Start by understanding how you store information. Study the following diagram to see how an incident in the outside world triggers your mind to immediately search for a reaction, a response which is therefore based on previously stored data:

Outside World	You	Inside World
Something Happens	You take it a certain way	It is stored that way as being what really happened regardless of facts

Outside World	"B" Mind	"A" Mind
Information ⟶ In	You use your "B" Mind to make your choice for you and then give that decision to your "A" Mind for storage	Your "A" Mind stores all information given to it the way it is presented and assumes that is the way you want it

Outside World	"B" Mind	"A" Mind
Something Happens ⟶	"B" Mind asks "A" for information to ⟶ find out what to do.	"A" searches storage to get information on the subject then
You do Something ⟵	"B" reacts immediately on the information given as true	gives whatever it finds to "B" for action

How does this work? Consider a fictional example. Suppose John, a supervisor, walks into a room filled with clerical employees who are hunched over computers. Rodney and Ellen are working side by side on one side of the room.

Rodney spies the supervisor and immediately becomes nervous. He has seen that look on John's face before, and he knows positively that it means bad news.

"Oh, no! He's coming over here towards me. Something's wrong. Maybe someone's going to get fired. I know I haven't been doing real well the past few weeks. And I've heard that we may go through a round of layoffs," Rodney thinks to himself. "How am I going to explain losing my job this time to my family?"

Working faster and faster, Rodney's frustration and nervousness become evident to anyone who looks. He knocks over a stack of papers. As he reaches over, red-faced, he readies himself with a "take this job and shove it" speech in case the axe falls on his head.

Ellen, at the same moment, sees her boss and wonders why he looks so enthusiastic.

"Great! He's coming over here towards me. I've heard that they are going to promote someone this week," she imagines. "I've really been doing well, and I know that my evening classes are finally going to pay off. Wow! I can't wait to tell my family about the new job."

It is the same supervisor, room and look on John's face. What is the difference in responses by Rodney and Ellen?

The varied reactions are triggered by storage in the A mind and the directions the B mind and body are given by that storage.

We can compare the mind switch to the inner workings of a computer, as outlined on the following page:

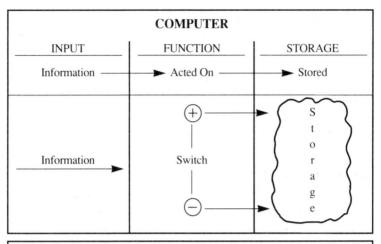

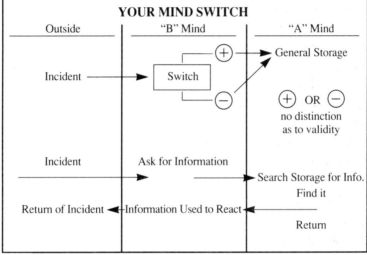

If you accept a misspelled word as truth, for example, it will pass through your mind switch, be stored and remain misspelled. When you see the word spelled correctly, your B mind pulls your interpreted spelling from your A mind and compares. At that moment, you must either edit the spelling by returning the correct version through your mind switch and into storage to replace the incorrect variation, or you will reject the correct spelling. Every time you store the incorrect version, accepting the correct spelling becomes increasingly more difficult.

Please understand — what is stored negative will come out negative. That is a fact throughout nature: if you plant a radish, if you harvest anything from that seedling, the chances are 100% that it will be a radish.

Your mind switch, a function of your B mind, is absolutely crucial to this entire process. It controls how every event, fact and emotion is interpreted as it passes into your A mind storage. Changing your mind switch is a rational, intellectual decision.

You have no control over some things in life, and little control over most other things. The one factor in life over which you have unequivocal mastery, if you choose to take control, is your mind switch.

But will you take control? As with so many other components of The Power Of Positive Doing, taking control of your mind switch is absolutely essential.

Mind-Switch Programming

Generally the human mind tends to be programmed towards the negative. For example, when the alarm goes off in the morning, most people don't have to force themselves to say, "Good grief, I'm tired. I wish I could just stay in bed. I just have a feeling that this is going to be a crummy day. My job — I just know there's going to be problems. And the economy — I wonder if it's going to take a nose dive." If you allow yourself to take the easy route, you can easily dwell on negatives most of the time.

Or you can force yourself to program positives. This goes so much deeper than so-called "positive thinking." It requires a conscious mind switching.

There is only one way to force yourself to accept, interpret and store information as positive input — you must jam your switch toward the positive, no matter what happens.

Here is the secret for doing that: when anything happens to you, say these magic words:

THIS IS THE GREATEST THING THAT EVER HAPPENED TO ME!

Is that crazy or what? Can you imagine saying those lines, even when something really bad takes place?

I was consulting for a company. The people in my seminars were all top executives, and when I met them for our first session, I discovered that they had just been dealt a stunning corporate blow. They had lost the largest contract in the history of their company, a project which would produce nearly 70% of their projected incoming cashflow.

That day I taught this principle of mind switch programming. Imagine the reaction I received when I encouraged these reeling executives to say, "This is the greatest thing that ever happened to me."

I got them to say it and they promised to repeat the sentence as homework between that time and our next session, but even as they left the class, I could tell that most of them were really thinking, "This is terrible. . .it can't get any worse. . .this is the worst thing that ever happened to us."

The CEO believed it, though, and after a few days of saying, "This is the greatest thing that ever happened to me," he began getting creative ideas. For starters, he

went to the head of the company which had not re-
newed the huge contract and asked, "Why?"

Later this executive told me:

> "I went with an open mind. I wanted to learn
> and correct whatever the situation was so that we
> wouldn't repeat the same mistakes. If I had not
> learned to say, 'This is the greatest thing that ever
> happened to me,' I would never have gone to see
> the man at the other company. I would have re-
> mained incredibly hurt, terribly mad and quite
> guilty. The company head saw that I had an open
> mind, and so he told me. We had lost the contract
> because of very good business reasons, but he
> could see that I was willing to work to correct the
> situations. Incredibly, I walked out of that meeting
> with signed contracts which were larger than the
> original ones we had lost and at a higher profit
> factor than the ones we had botched!"

During the past 30 years I have been very privileged
to teach men, women and children how to jam the mind
switch toward positive. I have seen a large percentage
of these people change the course of their lives by
learning to say, no matter what, "This is the greatest
thing that ever happened to me!"

A Final Note

Although she does not use the term, "mind switch," Louise Hay has touched millions of people with these words:

> "You are never stuck. This is where the changes take place, right here and right now *in our own minds*! It doesn't matter how long we've had a negative pattern or an illness or a poor relationship or lack of finances or self-hatred. We can begin to make a shift today! Your problem no longer needs to be the truth for you."[2]

You can change the interpretations of events and information which have been stored negatively in your A mind. You are the only person who has ultimate control of your mind switch. Your past thoughts and beliefs have created whatever you are this moment, and what you are now choosing to believe and think and say will create the next moment.

Wise philosophers and prophets throughout history have disagreed on nearly every major point, but on this point all great teachers have agreed — *you are what you think about.* Marcus Aurelius mused, "A man's life is what his thoughts make of it."

King Solomon wrote: "As a man thinks in his heart, so is he."

Ralph Waldo Emerson said this — "A man is what he thinks about all day long."

What do you choose? Do you allow your mind switch to flip over to the negative side when it is

---

2. Louise Hay, *You Can Heal Your Life* (Santa Monica, CA: Hay House, 1987), pp. 42-43.

convenient or "normal?" Or do you keep jamming the switch toward positive?

I can give you this great advice, coming from my years of experience, yet you can continue to choose to allow things to enter your mind through the negative switch. It is up to you. The principle of the power to choose works, but only if you work it!

You are the power in your own world. You will have whatever you choose to think.

And this very moment, right now, you can begin a new direction with your life. Your computer-like mind can only give back what you have stored in it, so begin to feed your A mind only through your positive mind switch.

Sure, that mind switch is rusty. Perhaps others will not understand. You may not FEEL (B mind) what you are forcing yourself to say. Say it anyway:

THIS IS THE GREATEST THING THAT EVER HAPPENED TO ME!

Then take action as though it *were* the greatest thing and watch what happens!

Positive +++♥++ Steps

(1) You can de-mystify the entire scope of how your mind works.

(2) Your mind is actually two spheres: the outer B mind and the inner A mind. When you understand how these two aspects of your mind work, The Power Of Positive Doing becomes even more of a step-by-step opportunity.

(3) Your B mind carries out the outside, intellectual functions — the way you dress, walk, comb your hair and act.

(4) Your A mind controls your emotional progress — the way you view yourself. What you do, consciously or subconsciously, is always directed by what you store in your A mind.

(5) Whatever the inside world is imagined to be is what the outside world will eventually become.

(6) You do not have to live as you now live. You can change not only the way your B mind interprets your world, but you can also change what is stored in your A mind.

(7) Jam your mind switch toward the positive by saying, no matter what occurs, "This is the greatest thing that ever happened to me." Then act that way.

Green Gorillas and *8*
Peeled Onions

Thank you for giving me
the tools to free me
from the tyranny of myself.

Thank you for turning on the lights
to the confusion—and
the beauty that's inside of me.

Thank you for showing me
that the only difference
between a plow horse
and a pegasus
is self-love.

—KATHIE PECK
YES Graduate

Taking Control

One of the most frightening, yet liberating feelings comes from realizing that YOU ARE IN CONTROL OF WHAT YOU THINK.

If you can see that, you can take charge of your life, your thought processes and your attitudes. That discovery, by itself, can de-mystify the entire scope of how your mind works. Once de-mystified, you begin to tap into The Power Of Positive Doing, and success becomes a step-by-step opportunity!

As mentioned before, not many people want to see how their emotions and mind works. Too many men, women and children want to keep everything cerebral shrouded in mystery or muddied by authoritarian-sounding words; then they can constantly blame someone else for their situations. How sad!

You can deal with life differently! Each of the previous chapters has focused on an important, but simplistic concept. Those chapters form the foundation for the structure which is being built from this point forward, beginning with an insightful look at ways to take control of your emotions.

LIFE AND STRESS

For each of the following questions, rate your job. Write answers in your notebook, using this scale:

0	Does not apply or never
1	Seldom
2	Sometimes
3	At least half the time
4	A majority of the time
5	Nearly all of the time

(1) Deadlines are a daily part of my job.

(2) When I leave my workplace, I generally complete work I have not had time to do during the workday (if yes, mark 5).

(3) Some of my co-workers are difficult to work with.

(4) I continue to allow myself to accept new job responsibilities without letting go of others.

(5) There is little variety or challenge in my job.

(6) I often feel overwhelmed with the demands of my life.

(7) When I am under pressure I tend to lose my temper.

(8) I have a problem completing work assignments because of the many interruptions.

(9) I am concerned with the goal of being a perfect employee, spouse and parent at the same time.

(10) My job is at home, so I cannot walk out and leave it at night (if yes, mark 5).

SCORING: Total your score for work/life stress. If your score is below 12, you are probably dealing effectively with the pressures of work and life.

If your score is between 13 and 30, you may be experiencing some physical or mental signs of distress.

If your score is over 30, work stress is signaling danger ahead. You must learn to handle your emotions immediately.

Adapted from C. Michele Haney, Ph.D., and Edmond W. Boenisch, Jr., Ph.D., *Stressmap: Finding Your Pressure Points* (New York: Impact Publishers, 1988), p. 487.

Basic Emotions

Anyone who has taken a beginning art course will tell you that there are three primary colors, from which dozens of shades radiate.

Likewise, though experiencing many varieties of feelings, every person possesses four basic emotions:

- MAD

- SAD

- SCARED

- GLAD

GLAD is the natural place to be, but the transition from GLAD to MAD is automatic when a real or imagined attack is experienced. There is no choice about this, and the condition cannot be reversed. From this point, MAD, SAD and SCARED must be experienced to be able to get back to GLAD.

MAD is a natural condition. It pours adrenaline into your system to help you instantly respond to challenges.

The transition from MAD to SAD can only be accomplished by doing something — by letting the anger flow.

SAD is the next natural state which is required to drain your system of all excess adrenaline. Excess adrenaline left in the system will eventually destroy you.

The transition from SAD to SCARED requires a decision: "Okay, so I am hurt — now I have to do something about it." You cannot stay in a state of SAD or depression. You must figure out what to do about your condition so that you can re-enter the world.

SCARED is also a natural condition. It requires withdrawal from your surroundings in order to feel sorry about the situation, to recuperate and to regain your perspective. It helps you figure out what to do next.

The transition from SCARED to GLAD requires a physical act. You must ask how long you can feel sorry for yourself before you decide to do the action you chose during SCARED.

GLAD, again, is the natural place to be. Once challenged, the synthesis begins again. Unfortunately, most people have no idea how this process works, nor do they know how to handle this emotion-clearing strategy.

Processing Emotions

Most of us are brought up to think that being angry is bad. Rather than teaching and modeling healthy ways to express anger, most authority figures teach repression or suppression of this natural emotion. As a result, we are a society of ticking time-bombs.

Kenneth R. Pelletier, Ph.D., author of *Mind as Healer, Mind as Slayer*, cites a number of studies regarding anger suppression. One researcher, examining the histories of more than 5,000 patients with rheumatoid arthritis, discovered that many of them shared certain personality traits, among them the inability to express anger.[1] Another scientist discovered that patients with ulcerative colitis produced strikingly comparable data to that of the rheumatoid arthritics, reports Dr. Pelletier.

Marjorie Brooks, Ph.D., a professor at Jefferson Medical College in Philadelphia, relates another study centering on the life history patterns of 400 cancer patients. Said Dr. Brooks:

> "They (the researchers) found the patients had some very interesting similarities. Many of them seemed unable to express anger or hostility in defense of themselves. The patients could get angry in the defense of others or in the defense of a cause. But when it came to self-defense, they didn't follow through. . . . Suppressed hostility was another significant factor appearing in some of the other patients. They seemed to lack the discharge mechanism needed to allow anger to surface, so they kept all of their anger inside."[2]

---

1. Emrika Padus, *Your Emotions & Your Health* (Emmaus, PA: Rodale Press, 1986), pp. 152-3.
2. Ibid, p. 153.

I don't suggest keeping the anger repressed, nor do I endorse lashing out at others when you are mad — far from it. According to Dr. Brooks, neither alternative is healthy. She often cites research on women undergoing breast biopsies:

". . .the women who were very, very seldom angry and women who were highly volatile were more likely to have malignant tumors than women who had an appropriate expression of anger."[3]

MADs often manifest themselves in terms of these physical or emotional distresses:[4]

Irritability	Muscle twitching
Loss of appetite	Frequent forgetting
Trouble sleeping	Heavy drinking
Headaches	Abuse of prescription drugs
Tired feelings	Asthma attacks
Overeating	Nausea or vomiting
Ringing in ears	Depression
Lump in throat	Minor accidents
Dry mouth	Cold hands or feet
Racing heartbeat	Sexual problems
Skin rashes	Feelings of resentment
Stomach pains	Constipation
High blood pressure	Nervousness
Nightmares	Heavy smoking
Allergy problems	Hyperventilation
Lower back pain	Infections

---

3. Ibid, P. 152.
4. Peter L. Brill, M.D., and John P. Hayes, Ph.D., *Taming Your Turmoil* (Englewood Cliffs, NJ: Prentice-Hall, 1981), p. 147.

Muscle aches/pains	Peptic ulcers
Indigestion	Dermatitis
Hives	Colitis
Menstrual Distress	Diarrhea

Obviously, venting anger is necessary for good health. Anger is a normal emotion that is a result of our genetics, upbringing and cultural patterns. The biggest problem we face is learning how to discharge it in a manner that is acceptable in society and healthy for the self.

The GLAD-MAD-SAD-SCARED-GLAD process, once recognized and nurtured, allows you to feel natural feelings. We are so thwarted that we have become rigid and unfeeling.

Listen to your mind. When something happens (such as a violation of RULE NUMBER ONE), let yourself *feel* angry. Don't retaliate immediately or verbalize your anger. Instead, go inside your mind and allow that anger to seethe. If you feel like hitting the person closest to you at the time, hit them over and over — but do it inside your mind. If you desire to "tell them off," go ahead — just do it inside your head instead of spewing your wrath outwardly.

If you can, let that MAD energy be used in constructive ways. It will scrub floors for you. It will build cabinets, wax woodwork, mow grass and shovel snow. Do something physical, whenever possible.

Mainly, let yourself *feel* the MAD. Don't just suppress it, ignore it or "blow your top." Get MAD — just learn how to make it work for you instead of destroying you.

Green Gorillas

How many times have you heard these phrases?

"When it happened, it made me so mad!"

"I could not believe how mad that woman forced me to be."

"Why are you always trying to set me off and make me mad?"

You don't GET mad; you ARE mad. If you have stored an event or piece of information negatively in your A mind, it can only come out in a negative form.

What if I came up to you and said, "Green Gorilla!" Would it mean anything? Probably not.

Would calling you a Green Gorilla make you mad at me? Not unless the label meant something negative to you.

But what if I walked up and said, "You big slob!" to a person who is overweight and has endured years of fatso-jokes? Of course, it would trigger an immediate and negative response. The person might not clobber me, but a MAD form (depression, hostility, self-pity, avoidance) will come to the forefront immediately.

Look again at the way your mind switch works, both as an event moves through your B mind into A mind storage, and then as it moves back through your B mind and causes a reaction:

GREEN GORILLA STORAGE

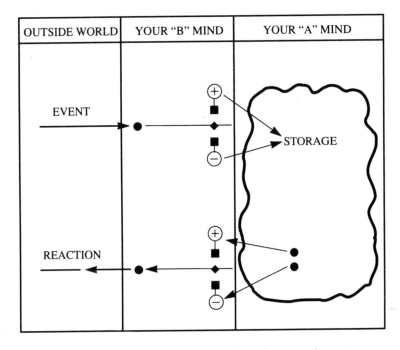

OUTSIDE WORLD	YOUR "B" MIND	YOUR "A" MIND

Your mind switch is yours. Therefore, only you can use it. Let me repeat again: YOU DON'T *GET* MAD, YOU *ARE* MAD. People don't MAKE you MAD unless you have something inside which has been stored negatively. While you cannot control outside "triggers," you can become a masterful Green Gorilla trainer.

What triggers your Green Gorillas?

Insults?

Raised eyebrows?

"If-only-you-would-have" scripts?

Rejections?

"Can't-you-be-more-like" comments

The Power of Positive Doing   137

Most of us have thousands of Green Gorillas stored inside. All it takes is the proper spark to provoke us:

- A child spills the milk, and the parent flies into a rage.

- A parent yells at the child, and the youngster shrieks in terror.

- A motorist honks at a jaywalker, and the red-faced pedestrian instantly curses loudly at the driver.

Wouldn't it be nice to live in a world where everyone knew how to deal with Green Gorillas? Again, you have no control over what other people do or how they react. You cannot change anyone else, but you can start with yourself by taking control of your not-so-imaginary, jade-colored primates.

Green Gorillas and Criticism

Criticism is rampant in business and industry (as well as everywhere else). No criticism is good; even so-called constructive criticism is actually destructive. It is human to err, and there are more humane ways to respond to the mistakes of others.

Suppose Sammy, an employee of yours, has managed to tip over one of the company trucks. There it is lying on its side with the embarrassed driver next to it. You walk up to him and ask, "How in the world could you do anything so stupid?" He already knows that rolling the truck over was hardly intelligent, so your diatribe is only going to add to the hurt feelings.

If you were in Sammy's shoes, how would you feel? What would your immediate response be if your boss walked up to you and began stating the painfully obvious facts?

You would naturally be defensive. You would say, "It wasn't my fault! It was that damn Green Gorilla walking down the street. The brakes didn't work, so I swerved to miss him and flipped the truck over. Don't yell at me!"

Use a different approach. Acknowledge diplomatically the fact that the truck is lying on its side. Don't scream, "Why did you turn the truck over the way you did?" Instead say, "Well, at least we can see now how worn the tires are."

Sammy knows you know that he made a mistake. Continue in an understanding manner. Establish an empathy, a rapport with him, and it will break down the defensive barriers.

If you don't break down the potential barriers at the beginning, you won't get anywhere. You will get more walls. People are generally tenacious when they must defend themselves. As a result, you may never find out what caused the problem or come up with a solution.

Ask questions — "How did it happen?" Then listen to Sammy's explanation. Don't get too serious. In truth, it really doesn't matter how it happened. That is now irrelevant. But act interested, even if you don't believe him. Don't keep interrupting and letting him know that you think he is wrong.

What you do say is, "What are you going to do now to correct this?" That is the question you really needed to ask from the moment you walked upon the scene of

The Power of Positive Doing   139

the overturned truck. You just had to build a bridge between you and Sammy to get to that point. What you really want to do is make sure it does not happen again.

Note the wording of that last question. Do not say, "What are you going to do next time so that this doesn't happen again?" That can be interpreted as a put-down. If you have a driver who is on the defensive and constantly being chased by assorted Green Gorillas, you will have a driver who stays frustrated, confrontational and accident-prone.

When Sammy tells you how he is going to correct the problem, listen very carefully. If you think that is the way to do it, say, "Go ahead." If you believe his plan will not work, then discuss it with him and probe other options. If he thinks his way is still better, you may have to ask him more questions and help him to understand how you desire for it to be done.

Remember, everybody is inherently good. Everybody wants to do a good job. So when people err and you treat them as if they wanted to do a bad job, you are setting the situation up incorrectly. You are also establishing a pattern for repeated failure.

Treat people as you would like to be treated. Listen very carefully. Avoid triggering their Green Gorillas. Involve them in the correction of the problem.

Reprocessing Your Green Gorillas

Processing your MADs (jamming your mind switch toward positive) is hard enough, but re-processing your stored MADs (Green Gorillas) can sometimes be much more difficult. Neither is impossible, however. In fact, as with all other principles found in The Power Of Positive Doing, there is a human parallel to the law of inertia. The more you do anything, the less difficult it becomes.

Reprocess the stored MADs. When someone triggers a MAD inside you, get MAD. When your A mind brings stored MADs to your consciousness, get MAD at the person in that brought-to-the-surface memory.

EXPERIENCE YOUR MAD, DO NOT EXPRESS YOUR MAD TO ANY ONE ELSE.

IT IS VERY IMPORTANT THAT YOU GET MAD AT THE MEMORY, NOT AT THE REAL PERSON

All MADs are stored as MADs, but if you process them from MAD to SAD to SCARED, you will be able to restore them as GLADs.

You are designed to be perfectly happy, totally euphoric and in love all the time. If you are not experiencing that level of life, it means that you have too many stored MADs.

If you get rid of all the Green Gorillas, nothing can set you off, no matter what happens. You would have the freedom to accept and love everyone.

Peeling Onions

We are forward-moving people, designed to be that way. We don't need to live in the past anymore. We should enjoy BEING and PLANNING.

When the same event keeps coming up in your mind, patterns of behavior or pictures of the past — pleasant or ugly — it is an unprocessed MAD. Give it up! Ask questions in your B mind.

And even when you deal with a MAD, you may discover that it is only the first layer of a core MAD. You may have to keep dealing with the MAD, taking off layer after layer, much as you would peel an onion.

Let me give you a very personal example. I love my father dearly, so it was quite unusual several years ago when I began getting pictures of him. It was a still photo. I knew enough to get mad at him to begin reprocessing whatever my A mind was telling me, but I didn't know why intellectually (B mind). As I dealt with the MAD, I began seeing more of the picture. My father was looking at me, and I was an 11 year old on a platform. I kept expressing anger until it would subside, then I would receive more information.

This reprocessing took most of a year, and though I would think that I had dealt with the MAD, it would keep resurfacing some time later.

Eventually, the still photographs became more like motion pictures, and went from a sepia-tone into vibrant color. Finally more and more of the scene became apparent to me — much of which I had long forgotten (or so I thought). Layer after layer of my core MAD "onion" melted away.

I was working at a coal and ice house. It was a summer job. I had been so proud of working a man's job and making good money, even though I was only 11 years old. He was telling me that I couldn't work there anymore: "Son, you're mama and grandmother are just afraid that this is too much for you, so you will have to quit working."

I realized just how much hatred I had built up against him. As I got mad, much as an 11 year old would, I was finally able to see how much he really loved me and wanted to protect me. It gave me an entirely new perspective of him.

It also helped me see why I had built up such resentment — why I had become an alcoholic at 13 years of age, constantly in trouble and continually manipulated by women.

It took me more than a year, but what a difference. Can you imagine the difference it can make in your life as you begin to deal with the MADs which surface in your mind? It can revolutionize every part of your life!

Just remember, you can only be genuinely mad at someone else. Your MAD comes from someone else out there, even if he or she doesn't know it or doesn't even exist. Recognizing that you are mad brings who you are mad at to the forefront. You've got to get mad at that person before you can get to SAD, SCARED and GLAD. By getting mad at the other person, it releases information in your A mind, which allows you to be aware of your original MAD. You can't get mad at yourself, only at others. When you feel mad long enough, the MAD will begin to dissipate. Then you can see more about yourself and what you should do. The Power Of Positive Doing helps you unlock that information by feeling your MAD.

A Final Note

Process your MADs by jamming your mind switch on the positive mode. Reprocess your MADs by allowing them to come from your subconscious (A mind) to the surface (B mind), where you can work through the MAD/SAD/SCARED/GLAD process.

Is it difficult? Yes, especially at first, but keep doing it.

Do you believe you deserve to have what you desire? Part of you probably does (your A mind), but your B mind probably keeps reminding you that you don't deserve better things and a MAD-free life.

Listen to your A mind! Treat your emotions and your processes with ultimate respect.

Put your knowledge of Green Gorillas to use in the workplace. Avoid triggering other people into defensive stances and repeated failures. Instead, treat them as you would like to be treated.

Positive +++♥++ *Steps*

(1) One of the most frightening, yet liberating feelings comes from realizing that YOU ARE IN CONTROL OF WHAT YOU THINK.

(2) Every person possesses four primary emotions: MAD, SAD, SCARED and GLAD.

(3) Processing those emotions allows you to experience natural, needed feelings: MAD ("Someone did something to me."), SAD ("I did it to me."), SCARED ("What do I do now?") and GLAD (I am taking positive action.")

(4) You don't GET mad; you ARE mad.

(5) All MADs are stored as MADs (Green Gorillas), but if you process them from MAD to SAD to SCARED, you will be able to restore them as GLADs.

(6) You may have to keep dealing with the MAD, taking off layer after layer, much as you would peel an onion.

(7) Experience your MAD, do not express your MAD to anyone else. It is very important that you get MAD at the memory, not at the real person.

Fill Your 9
Own Cup First

*My own success and happiness depends
    solely on me.*
*I must love myself first in order to truly
    love others.*
*The better I understand and accept my-
    self,*
*The more open minded and non-judge-
    mental I will become.*

—D. WOODWARD
YES Graduate

Love

A few years ago, enduring rock singer Tina Turner had another million-selling record with these lines:

"What's love got to do with it?
    What's love but a second-hand emotion?"

To some people, perhaps, a chapter about love seems out of place in a book written largely for business and professional people. "What's love got to do with it?" you may ask.

The basic premise of this book is to help you reach your full potential. In any capacity of life — business or otherwise — your goal should be to inspire yourself and those around you to higher levels. I believe this is the wave of the future, and the most visionary corporate leaders already understand this principle.

Too many people, however, view life as an opportunity to manipulate others into doing things. Too often management seeks to keep employees in check, and workers retaliate by reducing production to minimal limits. Or a salesperson may say, "If you buy from me, I'll be your good buddy, but if not, to heck with you!"

There is so much misunderstanding which hinges on the difference between love and anti-love. That is sad, for there is a significant place for love in the marketplace.

What Is Love?

Love is not a gushy word which describes a world of rose-colored-glasses, flowery bouquets and Shakespearean sonnets.

True, "love" is a word which is tossed around lightly today. Everywhere you turn, someone is using that word:

"I love my new car."

"I just love chocolate."

"Didn't you just love that movie?"

"I wish I could love my job more."

Love is the most basic component of life. Life *is* love. You can take the IF (uncertainty) out of life by replacing it with OV. OV is the Latin root for ovum, the egg. OV stands for the germ or seed of life. Therefore by superseding the skepticism, doubt and mistrust of IF with OV, a living nucleus, you have the dynamic word LOVE.

Imagine what would happen in the corporate world if uncertainty was removed from all communication, benefits, guidelines and systems, then replaced with a growing seed of belief, trust, aspiration and respect?

Love can only be love, however, if it is an action verb. It must be something that you do, not something that is done to you.

LOVE IS GIVING — nothing more, certainly nothing less. Some people call love a thought or a feeling. NOT SO! It is an action, and that action is giving in a special way. Love is not a sentimental attachment to a person. Love is a way of life, an attitude, a state of mind. Love does not come to you. Love comes from within you and you must give it out for it to exist.

A loving relationship is only possible when each person is free to live his or her own life, to set each other free and yet share without demanding. If I truly love you, then I give to you without strings. I give to you freely, not to make you change, be different or make you like me. If I truly love you, I accept you as you are. Then I can choose to associate with you or not based on my own value system. If I attempt to change you to agree with my value system, then I am not loving.

Love asks no return and seeks no reward. When you have it, people know you are not seeking anything from them. Their barriers go down. The more you love, the more people will gather around you who feel the same way.

When you truly love, it comes from your A mind. To give love and receive love is in our deepest nature, but a lot of us have been conditioned to think of love as something much less than it is.

Positive Doing Insights

LOVE

In your notebook write a sentence or two to explain your feelings about each question:

(1) As a child, how were you taught to love?

(2) Were your parents good examples of love-givers?

(3) What quality do you believe to be the most conducive to a loving relationship?

(4) What qualities do you believe to be the most destructive to a loving relationship?

(5) Are you able to give love freely — without strings?

(6) When are you unable to give love freely — without strings?

(7) Are you a good teacher of love-giving in your workplace, home and community? How?

NOTE: Your answers are YOUR answers. Are they the answers you want them to be?

Love is not a trade — "You do this and I will do that." Trades may be wonderful, but they aren't love. They are contracts.

Many of us learn to trade "love" at a very early age. A friend of mine in North Carolina tells of his two-year-old grandson who said, imploringly, "Paw Paw, if I crawl up in your lap and hug and all that stuff, will you read me a story?" That was a potential agreement between two people who may love each other, but it was not love.

We have been taught, quite innocently, through fairy tales about Prince Charming and Cinderella, that if you do all the right things, are pretty, smart, rich or cute, you will be loved and adored.

Many parents and teachers place such great importance on behavior and academic marks — "If you make good grades this semester, we will give you . . ."

Some dentists say, "Be a brave, nice kid and I will give you a lollipop!"

Songs through the years have also taught us wrong ideas about love:

> "Love me with all of your heart and I will
> love you."

> "I can't live if you don't love me."

> "Why won't you love me and make
> my life complete?"

Taking or giving with strings is not love. It is anti-love.

There is nothing wrong with a contract, trade or

agreement, but too often we make contracts, then we call them "love."

A woman in one of our sessions recalled one of her friends named Eve who had given gifts to a wealthy woman named Johna. Time after time Eve had done nice things for Johna, but she also kept admiring a gorgeous objet d'art. Finally she asked, "Johna, can I *buy* this beautiful piece from you?" Johna, nicely but firmly, said no. Later, when Eve was describing the event, she remarked to the YES student, "I just could not believe that she wouldn't sell it or give it to me — and *after all I've done for her!*"

Strings! Eve was using her gifts to be manipulative. When we manipulate, however, our "gifts" become a two-edged sword: "yes" makes you feel guilty and "no" makes you feel rejected.

We manipulate and become parasitic because we want a "yes!" With enough maturity, "yes" or "no" becomes okay.

Fill Your Own Cup First

This is a primary success tool — unless you learn to love yourself first, you cannot love anyone else.

Why?

Imagine your self as a cup. If you fill your self-cup to overflowing, you cannot keep from spilling all around yourself. If your cup is empty, you cannot share your resources with anyone else. It's that simple. FILL YOUR OWN CUP FIRST.

If you can love yourself first (and each of the strategies in The Power Of Positive Doing center on that wonderful purpose), other people will benefit greatly. It all starts with YOU.

If you don't love yourself, you will spend your life looking elsewhere for conditional love (anti-love), or as immortalized in Johnny Russell's song from *Urban Cowboy*, you will be "Looking for Love in All the Wrong Places." If you do not love yourself, you cannot give true love out to people, no matter how much you desire to do so.

For years we have heard the phrase from the Bible, "Love your neighbor as yourself," but we have wrongfully placed the emphasis on the neighbor. The statement is an equation. If you cannot love yourself first, there is no premise for loving your neighbor.

The cup must overflow everywhere. I must love everyone unconditionally, or I cannot love anyone.

The more you love yourself and fill your cup first, the more you have to give. Only when you love yourself can good things happen.

How do you love yourself?

I will be discussing other ways to love yourself in a subsequent chapter, but you can start by looking yourself in the mirror and saying, "I love and approve of myself." That is simple and easy enough, isn't it? Sure, you may feel foolish doing it, but who cares? If you do not love yourself, who will?

Find ways to compliment yourself. You have already had enough negative input into your A mind, so come up with creative positive input.

Love And Anti-Love

Love is very tangible. It is an action verb, an act of giving, an act of accepting and an act of helping people grow. Love is doing, as this comparison reflects:

TWO OPPOSING LIFE SYSTEMS

World of Anti-Love (What appears to be the Normal World)	World of Love (What I call the Natural World)
1. I am not in control of my environment.	1. I am in control of my environment.
Therefore, if I am not careful, someone will get me. This fills me with depression, worry, and confusion.	Therefore, no matter what happens, I will be able to take care of myself.
2. I live in a limited universe.	2. I live in an unlimited universe.
Therefore, I must get as much as I can. There is never enough to go around. If I give at all, it is only to get what I want. Ownership of people and things becomes important. I become afraid of others. I live in distrust.	Therefore, there will always be enough. I can afford to be generous because there is always more available. I don't have any reason to be afraid of others, so I don't have to feel separate or alienated. I live in trust.

3. Some people are more important than others.

   Therefore, a person has to have age, experience or credentials to be of value. The more one has, the more important he or she is.

3. Everybody is equally important.

   Therefore, because everyone has something to offer, anyone can be a student, teacher or whatever he or she chooses to be in life.

4. Love is always conditional.

   Therefore, I will love you if you conform and behave as I want you to.

4. Love is always unconditional.

   Therefore, it does not matter how the other person behaves or believes.

5. There are different kinds of love and varying degrees of love.

   Therefore, some people are worthy of my love and some are not. There are good people and bad people in the world. I must eliminate the bad people because I do not want them to hurt me or take things from me.

5. Love is love. There is only one kind and that is my acceptance of you for whatever you choose to be.

   Therefore, everybody is worthy of my LOVE (acceptance of them). This does not mean that I have to associate with you if I choose not to; still, I have no right to eliminate you.

6. The past predicts the future.

   Therefore, because there has always been war, hate and pestilence, sooner or later I am going to be attacked. To protect myself, I should attack first.

6. Anything and anybody can change.

   Therefore, the past does not necessarily predict the future. I can work constructively today to create a peaceful world here and now.

7. Love is limited and terminal. What we do dies when we do.

   Therefore, what I do is not important. What you see is what you get.

7. Love is limitless and goes on forever. The things we do live beyond us.

   Therefore, everything I do is important. There is more to life than meets the eye.

8. Everything around me is separate from me.

   Therefore, how I feel about the people and events in my life is what I think those people and events really are, and their actions and effects have nothing to do with me. They will never change.

8. Everything around me is a mirror of me.

   Therefore, how I feel about the people and events in my life is a reflection of what is going on inside of me. As I change, they will change in their relation to me.

9. The world is a terrible place filled with pain, frustration, unhappiness and depression.

   Therefore, I will cope with life and put up the difficult times.

9. The world is a beautiful place filled with wonder, excitement, challenge and happiness.

   Therefore, I will enjoy all of my experiences, even the difficult ones.

10. Happiness comes from something or someone else.

    Therefore, I will "love" with strings and be a manipulator so that something or someone will make me happy.

10. Happiness comes when I become a truly loving person.

    Therefore, I will love without any strings, conscious that happiness comes from my inner self, not from outward consequences.

If I love you, do I do it for you or me? If it is true that for me to grow as a person I must love, then I am giving to you for me. Whatever benefits spill over onto you — that is fine, too. But I love you for my own benefit.

Love is an active verb — not passive. It is something you and I DO; it is not something which is done to us.

A Final Note

Love is not some esoteric, hearts-and-flowers mirage. It is an active verb. Love is real life. And the more you learn to give without strings, the more you will have to give.

Love starts with you. Love yourself first. Fill your own cup first. Then let it overflow so that you can keep filling your cup more and more. This is a universal principle which keeps your self-cup fresh and pure, not stagnant.

You have a special privilege, a responsibility, to be all that you are, even if what you really are is not compatible with what you have learned to be (because of NSIs). You have a right to those feelings, even if those feelings are frowned upon or misunderstood by others.

You, alone, are responsible for living your life and for your own happiness and contentment. You cannot live totally for others (which makes you a taker), nor can you use others for your own self-affirmation.

You cannot be happy being what you think others want you to be, for what they want usually is not what you are.

You must accept and love yourself as you are before you can accept and love others.

Most people's lives have become jumbled and tangled like knotted fishing line. The walls that you have created to protect those knots end up isolating you from life. These walls and tangles need to be undone.

Have you ever untangled a fishing line or knocked down a wall? Viciously attacking either the snarled line or the barricade usually doesn't work very well. If anything, bombardment makes things worse. You may even get hurt.

You are much too important to attack your own snarls or walls. You are special. Be very gentle and understanding of yourself as you untangle your life and remove the walls of isolation.

Be patient with yourself. Your A mind wants to show you more of yourself and your potential if you will only let it.

Above all, love what you are becoming through the process. The willingness to let go of the old, past hurts is the key in *The Power Of Positive Doing*.

Positive +++♥++ Steps

(1) Love is an action verb, not passive.

(2) Love is giving without strings — an outpouring that needs no return because it is its own reward.

(3) Taking or giving with strings is not love, it is anti-love.

(4) Unless you learn to love yourself first — to fill your own cup first — you cannot love anyone else.

(5) Begin loving yourself by saying, "I love and approve of myself," and by giving heartfelt compliments to your self.

Listen Your Way **10**

To Success
(Hunches and Intuition)

"To learn that I can have
    whatever I want
      has been a revelation.
Also, to learn that nothing
    comes into my life
    unless I ask for it
       REALLY has put me
       on my toes.
If something appears that I don't like,
    I turn within to find out why.
It has been interesting to discover
    that in so doing
       the situation clears up
       as soon as my thinking is right
I listen to the inner voice,
    and I am guided by the inner voice.

Life is beautiful,
    life is full
       and I am happier
       than I have ever been."

—EVELYN WILKS
YES Graduate

Intuition

Intuition is defined by Webster as "the art or faculty of knowing directly, without the use of rational processes." Most of us have intuitive flashes — we call them "hunches," "our sixth sense," "gut feelings" or "an inner voice." We receive these signals many times during the day and night:

- We like someone immediately.

- We're suspicious of someone else without knowing why.

- An inner voice tells us that one decision is better than another.

Perhaps we should listen more to these feelings. In the past, rational thinkers have called these intuitions that later proved correct "lucky guesses" or flukes. More and more, however, intuition is finding new respect among both men and women, particularly in the corporate boardrooms. Intuition has always been a well-used tool of successful sales and marketing people.

Intuition is a tool which should be used by all people — from business executives to office workers, from educators to students. Your A mind is infused with universal wisdom, but you must be willing to accept and utilize it.

How do you rate in this area?

Positive Doing Insights

INTUITIVE INSTINCTS

In your notebook write the letter which denotes your answer, then add a sentence explaining why:

(1) When I don't have a ready answer, I tend to be:
    (a) patient.
    (b) clumsy.

(2) When working on a difficult problem, I usually:
    (a) concentrate on finding the solution.
    (b) play around with the possibilities.

(3) In most cases, change:
    (a) makes me nervous.
    (b) is exciting to me.

(4) I prefer to be told:
    (a) exactly how to do things.
    (b) only what needs to be done.

(5) When faced with a task, I usually:
    (a) create a plan before starting.
    (b) plunge right in.

(6) When describing something, I usually rely on:
    (a) analogies and anecdotes.
    (b) facts and statistics.

(7) When I disagree with others, I usually:
    (a) let them know it.
    (b) keep it to myself.

(8) When my intuition differs from facts, I usually:
    (a) trust my feelings.
    (b) follow the logical course.

(**Scoring** — the closer you are to the following answers, the more intuitive you are:1-a, 2-b, 3-b, 4-b, 5-b, 6-a, 7-a, 8-a.)

Power Of Your A Mind

Can people actually increase their powers of intuition?

"Absolutely!" says psychologist Weston Agor, a University of Texas-El Paso professor who conducts intuition training seminars for business executives. Here, condensed, are three of his suggestions:[1]

(1) **Set aside time for quiet contemplation.** Do this every day as well as just before making an important decision.

(2) **Pay more attention to mental images.** Sometimes an intuitive message is fleeting. If you are not receptive, you won't notice it.

(3) **Take a sheet of paper, and in the middle of the page, write down and circle a word that seems central to a problem.** What associations does it evoke? As you jot down seemingly random words and phrases around the center, a pattern and focus may emerge.

Intuition — use it! Develop it! You are going to need it more and more as you live in an increasingly complicated world.

1. *Working Smart* (Stamford, CT: Learning Systems, 1987).

Practical Steps

To get your inner voice working, you must want it. You must devote time to it. You have to practice "letting go" to test your intuition.

Intuition requires absolute honesty, for without it, you may interpret your thoughts wrongly.

Join your A mind with others. Just as the more you love, the more you attract loving people around you, so it is true that the more you tap into your universal wisdom, the more you will come into contact with intuitive, positive people.

A Final Note

Judy Fuller, a recent YES graduate, told of something that has become very common among her colleagues. She said:

"One very rainy day, I rode into Boston with my family to see an exhibition of some paintings by my daughter-in-law, an artist of growing reputation. Since it was raining so hard, I began visualizing a parking space within a short walking distance of the gallery. I kept saying to myself, 'We'll drive up to the door and find a space.' This was in a very busy area, Newbury Street. Wouldn't you know it — as soon as we drove up to the address, a car pulled out of a parking space, leaving it vacant, and right in front of the gallery door!"

There is no way Judy's B mind could have known that the parking place would be open, but she was willing to get past her intellectual screen and into her A mind. You can, too!

Put your A mind to use, whether you are at home, in the workplace or in any setting. You have an incredibly potent "perennial knowledge" within you. You can choose to build that mastery as you integrate your intuitive wisdom with the other strategies you are learning in The Power Of Positive Doing.

Use it!

Positive +++♥++ Steps

(1) Most of us have intuitive flashes — we call them "hunches," "our sixth sense," "gut feelings" or "an inner voice."

(2) Intuition is a tool which should be used by all people — from business executives to office workers, from educators to students.

(3) Your A mind is infused with universal wisdom, but you must be willing to accept and utilize it.

(4) To get your inner voice working, you must want it. You must devote time to it. You have to practice "letting go" to test your intuition.

Talk Your Way *11*
To Success
(Self-Speech)

"As I walk along the water's edge
   Making impressions on the sand.
The waves that roll up in front of me
   Prepare a new surface for me to see.
Ready for the next impression by me,
   The next wave leaves a new surface
       for all to see.
Something has changed, that impression
   That was put there by me,
       left a change for eternity.
The visible mark is gone.
   The sand is the same.
       The sea is the same.
The change was made by me."

—GIL ADAMS
YES Graduate

Building Value

Over and over again I have tried to help you understand what an amazing person you are. You can accept
that fact or you can ignore it. Regardless, *you are important*. You have value. I hope you will accept that
fact!

Granted, realizing your importance requires a major
life-adjustment. If you enjoy being a victim, you may
not want to change the cycle. Mistreatment allows you
to wallow in self-pity, which is very comfortable to
many people.

Can you imagine how much stress and worry would
be removed from your life if you only realized how important you are?

Worry comes from the belief that you are powerless.
You are not powerless. Granted, you are only one of
five billion people living on this globe, but there is a
reason for your existence. You have more than enough
natural intelligence and ability within you to reach any
goal you want to achieve — whether it is a business
goal or a personal ambition.

You are important! Say the words of RULE NUM-
BER ONE outloud:

I AM IMPORTANT.

Now the secret is to get your inner self to believe
those words.

The Power Of Self-Speech

You talk to yourself constantly, whether you realize it or not. You have undoubtedly talked, verbally or internally, as you have been reading the pages of this book:

"Let's see if I can understand what Ivan means by that."

"How can he say that?"

"That's what I have always felt."

"I need to remember that."

Most of the time people are not aware that they are talking to themselves. It just comes automatically. You are talking to yourself nearly every moment of every day.

This language of the mind can be controlled to work for us, to help make us into the people we want to be. King Solomon, whose name is synonymous with wisdom, wrote, "Death and life are in the power of the tongue" (Proverbs 18:21). Whatever you speak out of your mouth influences your thoughts.

The Roman philosopher Seneca once said, "Speech is the index of the mind." Jesus Christ put it this way, "Out of the abundance of the heart the mouth speaks." Whatever you begin focusing on is what you speak, and whatever you speak, your mind believes. The spoken word reinforces the image in your mind and ultimately that mental picture will probably become reality.

Children are good at making their thoughts come alive, though not always in a positive way. How many times have you seen a youngster speak sickness into existence. If he or she doesn't want to go to school, for whatever reason, that child will find a way not to go, looking listless, drooping shoulders, saying, "Mom, I don't feel well. My stomach hurts and I think I have a temperature."

Mom doesn't help by saying, "Well, maybe you're coming down with the flu or getting a bad cold."

By the next morning, it is no surprise that the child really does have a scratchy throat and a rising temperature.

By adulthood, most of us have become very good at manipulating our minds and bodies.

Have you ever heard someone say, "I just can't lose weight. I've tried every diet that ever came along, but I don't lose. I gain." And they do!

What about these self-zingers:

- "I'm always late to everything."

- "Every time I open my mouth I just seem to put my foot in it."

- "People just don't like me at all."

- "I'm always so tired."

- "I can't sit in a draft, 'cause I'll catch pneumonia."

- "Business is always crummy this time of year."

- "My boss is always on my case. Nothing I do seems to please her."

- "My employees just don't care about quality anymore."

The Power of Positive Doing

People get what they keep telling their A mind that they want. Change your self-speech and you can change your life. This is one of the most potent strategies in The Power Of Positive Doing.

Universal Law

People generally get what they desire, and those desires surface in the form of self-speech. Somehow, a person's words unconsciously tap into his or her deepest desires.

This is true with all universal laws. Whether you understand gravity or not, it will destroy you if you jump from a skyscraper ledge or it will help you as you build muscles.

You may not be able to explain how electricity works, but the power which surges through the wires in your home can kill you or enhance your life.

Charles Capps, in his best-selling book, *The Tongue, A Creative Force*, shares this thought-provoking analogy:

> "A few years ago I came upon the scene of an accident. A car had gone out of control and cut off a power pole. The high line wire was hanging about three feet above the ground. Many people had stopped and gotten out of their cars. They were standing no more than three feet away from that live wire, thinking that it was insulated, or that the power was *cut off*. But this was not true, the wire was *"live"* with over 17,000 volts of electricity. I watched from my car, a safe distance away, as the ambulance attendants carried a woman on a

stretcher up the highway embankment. As they crawled under the powerline one of them got too close, and the electrical current *arced* to his body like a lightening bolt. He died instantly and the other attendant was critically injured.

"He violated the natural law that governs electricity. No doubt he did it in ignorance, yet it was fatal. Lack of knowledge did not stop the electrical force. It continued to work. It was the same force that cooked his meals, heated his house, and washed his clothes. It was created to work for him to make life more enjoyable. The very reason for its existence was to supply his needs, but when he violated the law that controlled that force, it destroyed him."[1]

Likewise, whether you understand the dynamics of self-speech, this universal law is constantly at work in your life. Your words are unceasingly planting seeds in your A mind.

What are you saying to yourself?

---

1. Charles Capps, *The Tongue — A Creative Force* (Tulsa, OK: Harrison House, 1976), p. 10.

Negatives To Overcome

Why don't people use the potent power of self-speech in a more positive way?

Perhaps a better question is to ask why so many people use their self-speech as a negative force? The answer is related to the fact that we are taught, by an overwhelming margin, to be negative. Because of NSI programming, your mind switch always tends to go negative.

Consider these shocking statistics from acclaimed psychologist Shad Helmstetter:

> "During the first eighteen years of our lives, if we grew up in fairly average, reasonably positive homes, we were told 'No!,' or what we could *not* do, more than 148,000 times .... Meanwhile, during the same period. The first eighteen years of your life, how often do you suppose you were told what you can do or what you can accomplish in life? A few thousand times? A few hundred? During my speaking engagements to groups across the country, I have had people tell me they could not remember being told what they could accomplish in life more than three or four times! Whatever the number, for most of us the 'yes's' we received simply didn't balance out the 'no's'."[2]

Dr. Helmstetter reveals these shocking statistics:

- According to leading psychologists, psychiatrists and researchers in the behavioral sciences, as

---

2. Shad Helmstetter, Ph.D., *What to Say When You Talk to Your Self* (New York: Simon & Schuster/Pocket Books, 1986), p. 20.

much as 77% of everything we think is detrimental and negative.[3]

- At the same time, researchers in the medical field say that as much as 75% of all diseases and disorders are self-induced.[4]

NSIs and "elephant stakes" abound! These figures show that as much as 75% or more of our programming is the harmful, negative kind. Year after year our thoughts have been influenced wrongly. We have, in effect, become our own worst enemies.

How do we turn the power of self-speech around and begin programming ourselves to understand how magnificent and important we really are?

Beyond Positive Thinking

In my consulting and counselling work, most of the people with whom I work want to be successful, but they are frustrated. They often tell me, "I do all the right things — positive thinking and self-motivation and seminars, but nothing seems to work over the long haul."

As I mentioned in the beginning of this book, I do believe in positive thinking. I believe in success motivation. My work involves both of those exciting, dynamic principles.

---

3. Ibid, p. 21.
4. Ibid.

But, as I have pointed out so many times through the pages of The Power Of Positive Doing, true change must come from the inside out.

Your desire to change can fail because of one or more of these common reasons:

- Failure to take personal responsibility.

- Blaming others for your lack of success.

- Unwilling to pay the price for achievement.

- Thinking that the price for change is too excessive.

- Floundering when the challenge gets too steep.

- Deciding, halfway into the problem, that your desire to succeed wasn't quite so important after all.

- Being unsure about your goals, especially when compared to the current comfort zone.

Your successes in life are determined by what you DO. What you DO is motivated by your A mind. Your A mind is governed by your programming.

Therefore, to transform your life — to alter your actions and become a POSITIVE DOER, you must change your programming. You have to take the responsibility for internal coding!

Upgrading Your Level Of Self-Speech

You can program yourself constructively by verbally painting a new internal picture of yourself, sketching yourself as you want to be through positive self-speech.

You can move from negative acceptance ("I can't") and the recognition of a need to change ("I need to" or "I should") — both of which are harmful forms of self-programming — to positive action-talk ("I no longer," "I am" and "I have").

There are hundreds of innovative ways you can program yourself with positive self-speech. Here are a few examples you can use:

"I love and approve of myself."

"I am at peace with myself."

"I am in control of my life."

"I am a unique and special human being."

"I am proud of all my accomplishments in life."

"I am achieving my financial goals."

"I am successful."

"I am organized and in control of my life."

"I am healthy and slender."

"I have a great memory."

"I have no habits that hold me back from my true potential."

The Power Of Positive Doing explodes when you discover the potential of positive self-speech. You will begin to deal with challenges and opportunities in an entirely fresh, creative, self-actualizing manner. Positive self-speech strengthens, electrifies, asserts and activates you toward success — from the inside out!

Create Success By Speaking Success

Louise Hay, in her wonderful book, *You Can Heal Your Life*, offers many universal affirmations, such as this:

"In the infinity of life where I am, all is perfect, whole and complete. I recognize my body as a good friend. Each cell in my body has Divine Intelligence. I listen to what it tells me, and know that its advice is valid. I am always safe, and Divinely protected and guided. I choose to be healthy and free. All is well in my world."[5]

As you move up the levels of positive self-speech, consider these guidelines for creating your personal affirmations:

- When you catch yourself making negative statements, stop and turn them into positive self-speech. Instead of saying, "I am afraid to . . ." say, "I really enjoy . . . ."

---

5. Louise L. Hay, *You Can Heal Your Life* (Santa Monica, CA: Hay House, Inc., 1984), p. 147.

- Always phrase your self-speech statements with "I," making them very personal and meaningful.

- Keep your self-speech in the present tense. Make it true for you now, not in the future or in the past. Especially be careful about saying, "I am going to . . ." since you will likely never get to that point. A present-tense form of self-speech allows you to experience — right now — what it will be like once you actually realize your dreams.

- Make your self-speech statements enjoyable and exciting. Let your words fill all your needs and desires.

- Write your self-speech statements, perhaps using the notebook you have kept for each chapter's POSITIVE DOING INSIGHTS. By writing these sentences, you develop your ideas and self-image enhancers. Those thoughts will influence your actions.

- Use a mirror, as often as possible, when you make your positive self-speech statements.

- Practice loving yourself with positive self-speech at least a few minutes each morning, night and sometime during the day. Become your own best friend and encourager!

Do it! You will be surprised at how amazing, responsive and wonderful you really are.

POSITIVE SELF-SPEECH STATEMENTS

In your notebook, re-write these 10 common expressions into better self-scripts:

(1) I just don't have enough time in the day to get to the really important things.

(2) I'm so overweight, but I just can't seem to lose those extra pounds.

(3) Today's inflation rate is really killing us little guys.

(4) I guess I'm just meant to be this way.

(5) I really should be more of a giving person, but I just don't seem to have any extra money.

(6) I am always so mixed-up.

(7) My job is rotten . . . things just aren't going very
     well for me at work.

(8) I'm so disorganized.

(9) I'm just so afraid of failing when I face new chal-
     lenges.

(10) I only wish I could . . .

A Final Note

When you discover positive self-speech, you begin planting first rate seeds in your A mind. You also start pouring wealth principles into your life.

Use positive self-speech affirmations for three weeks, and your life will change forever!

Such statements make you feel successful, proud of yourself and very hopeful about life. Discovering the secrets of governing, administering and routing the untapped resources of your A mind is the greatest challenge any of us will ever face.

Positive self-speech furnishes the dynamic difference between success and emptiness.

The difference rests inside you! Talk to yourself. You are important (RULE NUMBER ONE), so treat yourself with honesty and respect (RULE NUMBER TWO).

When you tap into the power of positive self-speech, you give yourself one of the greatest, most unlimited gifts in the entire universe!

Love yourself. Give yourself good affirmations. Plant positive seeds in your A mind. Your life will never be the same!

Positive +++♥++ *Steps*

(1) Your brilliant inner self, coupled with your fantastic body, form a magnificent system which is capable of achieving unlimited accomplishments.

(2) You program your inner self through either positive or negative self-speech.

(3) Positive change must come from the inside out.

(4) To transform your life, you must change the level of self-speech from "I can't" to "I am" and "I have."

(5) You are important (RULE NUMBER ONE), so treat yourself with honesty and respect (RULE NUMBER TWO). Positive self-speech gives you this unlimited opportunity.

Give Your Way *12*
To Success

Success	*Failure*
Goals	*Poles*
Happiness	*Unhappiness*
Acceptance	*Rejection*
Love	*Anti-love*
Giving	*Taking*

Which stairway do you prefer?
It's up to you!

—A. A. BLAKE
YES Graduate

To Give Or Not To Give?

We live in a narcissistic world, where "do unto others as you would have them do unto you" often seems more like a fairy tale than a life-principle.

How sad! A lot of people are missing out on one of the greatest strategies for success.

Through much trial and error, I have learned that giving unselfishly of money and time unleashes a universal law. When you learn to practice the 10/10 rule (which I will explain), you will be pleasantly surprised at:

- The deepening and strengthening of your A mind powers.

- The increased abilities you will have in meeting your "regular" obligations.

- The creative ways you will move from giving a smaller amount to a larger amount.

- The preparation this gives to be a faithful and wise steward over your growing financial base.

In fact, most of the thousands of people that I know who have put the 10/10 rule into effect usually say, "I only wish I would have learned this principle a long time ago!"

What do I mean by the 10/10 rule?

It is very simple. Give 10% of your earnings and time to yourself first, then give an additional 10% of your time and earnings to others — unselfishly!

The principle you learned with love — that it is an active verb — carries over to the strategy of giving.

GIVING

In your notebook, write your answers and a candid explanation for those conclusions:

(1) Are you good at giving compliments to others?

(2) Are you good at receiving compliments from others?

(3) Can you pick out one special time when you gave unselfishly to someone whom you knew could never repay you or return the favor?

(4) What are your biggest hindrances to giving more money or time to others?

Pay Yourself First

In addition to 10% of your time you should be giving to yourself (loving, giving compliments and pampering yourself), you should begin to pay 10% of all your earnings to yourself FIRST.

Put this amount from each paycheck in a no-touch account — saving, CD, mutual funds, IRA — which you can build and then use for collateral in investments.

Keep investing it and don't touch. Let it grow and accumulate.

Give To Others

The second part of the 10/10 law means that you should give 10% of your time and money to others.

"That's ridiculous!" you say. "I don't have enough money to live on as it is."

If you don't have enough money to pay your bills anyway, why not do it for a few weeks? What do you have to lose? What if it really works?

The secret: there can be no strings. Give it to someone or a charity where they don't know who gave it.

This one action can plant many great things which will be harvested for the rest of your life!

You are never going to know what will happen until you make yourself do it.

Keri attended the YES course nearly five years ago. At that time she was on welfare. She came to me after the 10/10 session and said, "I can't believe you expect me to do this! I can't pay my bills. I'm trying to raise two children by myself. I like everything else that you have taught, but this is ridiculous."

I smiled and said, "Have I led you wrong on any of the other strategies?"

"No," she admitted. "I am really making some good changes and am taking responsibility for my choices. Even other people are noticing the difference."

"Then why would I start to lead you wrong now?" I asked. "I wouldn't share anything that would hurt you, and it is something that has revolutionized my life."

We talked a few more minutes, and Keri decided that she had nothing to lose except 20% (10% for herself and 10% for others) of next to nothing.

That next week she got a large amount of groceries delivered to her doorstep from a person she hardly knew. The following week she landed a job as a waitress in a very nice restaurant. More exciting was the fact that she began receiving four times more tips than the other waitpersons, night after night.

Keri soon was boosted to a managerial job. Her career has since continued to climb steadily.

Was it coincidence? I might believe that myself if I had not seen this principle work time after time. I cannot explain it, but I know that it works.

The more creative your giving becomes, the better it works. Put $10 bills into separate envelopes and leave them where your A mind tells you. Go up to strangers, especially when your A mind suggests, and hand them a gift. You cannot believe how liberating this is. Just remember, there can be no strings for it to be a true gift!

Giving 10% does not involve money alone. You can volunteer time to a church or charity, give a few hours a week to listening to someone talk, offering a shoulder to cry on, taking a lonely person to lunch, helping a civic organization or a hospital with a fund-raising effort.

On a personal note, learning to give time and money

in totally unselfish ways transformed me from a taker to a giver, and I received an unusual benefit that I never expected — I no longer have arthritis! I have since learned (from such teachers as Louise Hay) that arthritis is often a "taking" disease, caused by feeling unloved, resentful and victimized.

It can work for you, too, if you keep testing to make sure that there are absolutely no strings.

The Biology Of Caring

Let me emphasize the matter of giving 10% of your time, for it is vitally important to your future.

Everyone receives an equal supply of time. The only difference between us is the way we spend it. Each week brings us 168 golden hours. We spend approximately 56 hours for sleep and recuperation. We spend approximately 28 hours for eating and personal duties. We spend approximately 40 to 50 hours for earning a living.

We have 30-40 hours left to spend just as we wish. How do we spend them? How many hours for recreation? How many hours watching television? How many hours do you give to others?

For years, prominent scientists have believed that giving unselfishly of yourself to others is an effective antidote to the stresses of life. One of them, the late Hans Selye, M.D., who was responsible for the early studies tying stress to illness, called the concept "altruistic egoism."

Biblical scholars might call it the "As ye sow, so shall ye reap" syndrome.

Regardless, it seems that unselfish generosity has valuable paybacks:

- Giving feeds your A mind with positive seeds.

- Giving builds a heightened self-esteem.

- Giving causes love and gratitude in return (although this should not be the purpose, or it involves anti-love strings).

- Giving inspires those we help to help others.

- Giving offers a cumulative source of good feelings about life.

How important is giving to your self, inwardly and outwardly?

Psychiatrist George Vaillant, M.D., director of a 40-year study of Harvard graduates, identified unselfish altruism/giving as one of the qualities that helped even the most poorly adjusted men of the study group deal successfully with the stresses of life.[1]

Moreover, James Lynch, Ph.D., a leading specialist in psychosomatic medicine from the University of Maryland School of Medicine, documented the connection between selfishness/loneliness and heart disease. He writes:

"The mandate to 'Love your neighbor as you love yourself' is not just a moral mandate. It's a psychological mandate. Caring is biological. One thing you get from caring for others is that you're

1. George Vaillant, M. D., *Adaptation to Life* (New York: Little, Brown & Co., 1983), p. 235.

not lonely. And the more connected you are to life, the healthier you are." [2]

Alfred N. Larsen has seen evidence of that firsthand. Larsen is national director of the federal Retired Senior Volunteer Program (RSVP), which regularly places over 250,000 elderly people in community volunteer jobs. Larsen says he is convinced of the value of volunteer work for all people, especially the elderly who lose family, friends and often a purpose for life as they grow older. He insists:

> "Doctors always tell us that elderly people who engage in volunteer work are a lot better off, visit the doctor less often and have fewer complaints."[3]

What do you want from life? Are you willing to give at least 10% of your money and time to yourself and others?

Remember, if you plant positive seeds, you will reap a positive harvest.

---

2. James Lynch, Ph.D., *The Broken Heart: The Medical Consequences of Loneliness* (New York: Basic Books, 1987), p. 169.
3. Emrika Padus, *Your Emotions & Your Health* (Emmaus, PA: Rodale Press, 1986), p. 123.

So you want to be happy, healthy and live a long life? Practice the 10/10 rule.

Does that mean that you have to give away 90% of everything you make, as did the late earth-moving machinery tycoon R. G. LeTourneau?

Does that mean you must become a modern-day Albert Schweitzer or Mother Theresa?

Must you turn your business over to associates and become involved in mission field work, as Domino's Pizza founder Tom Monaghans did?

Or, does it mean that you have to become a "doormat" for people who beg for your money or attention.

No! Giving is another form of anti-love if you are only giving to get something in return.

The only way a giver can really reap the benefits of giving is if the urge comes from the goodness, not the need, in his or her heart.

If you are giving because of the emotional "goodies" you get out of it, you are not really giving. If you get angry because the person you have helped doesn't thank you, you are still giving with strings attached.

Give of yourself and your pocketbook, but give for the right reasons. Imagine what a difference it would make if every American gave an average of 2.5 hours a week to volunteer or charity work; it would be equivalent to mobilizing an army of 20 million full-time volunteers!

Our country could become a therapeutic community, one in which the problems of the world could be largely alleviated.

Who knows what can happen as more and more people tap into the mastery within?

That, in the end, is my hope — a world of wise,

mature, loving/giving men, women and children. When we learn the secret of giving, we will propel ourselves significantly toward happiness and healthiness.

May you be a catalyst in this movement as you continue to use the strategies in The Power Of Positive Doing.

Just remember, give 10% to yourself first, then give 10% to others.

Positive ✚✚✚♥✚✚ *Steps*

(1) We live in a narcissistic world, but you can learn to unleash a universal law by practicing the 10/10 principle.

(2) Give 10% of your time and money to yourself first.

(3) Give 10% of your time and money to others — without any strings attached.

(4) Even though you should not give to get, you will keep discovering that unselfish generosity has valuable paybacks — in every area of your life.

Afterword

Success Is . . .

For each one, what is his measure of success?
The most tender steak in town?
Artistic cake decoration?
Exotic scents and sophisticated colors?
Money? Limelight? Friends?

Something is happening in this valley
To people who want success in their lives;
Having love poured all over them,
With time and money to do whatever they want to do.
How to achieve it? Ah —
They are learning to take a look at themselves,
Learning how to program their own lives:
Learning to listen,
Learning to process emotions,
Learning to process negatives,
Learning to be givers, not takers,
Learning that we are what we let ourselves be.

Class graduation is a shared dinner and shared joys.
Graduates are members of a very special club
With no dues and no meetings,
With a new sense of awareness
And a knowledge that any goal can be achieved.
We become what we think about:
Rich man, poor man, beggar man, thief,
Doctor, lawyer, merchant, chief.

—DOROTHY SCHMIDT
YES Graduate

What Do You Want?

Do you want enough time? Do you want plenty of money? Do you want to be able to know how you should live, day by day? Do you want to be successful?

You can create your own success, not just with what you know, but by what you DO!

- Ask yourself, "How much do you want success?"

- Realize that there are no accidents.

- Live by RULE NUMBER ONE — you are important.

- Practice RULE NUMBER TWO — absolute honesty.

- Unlearn Negative Supportive Information.

- Be a goal-setter, not a POLE-sitter.

- Go beyond positive thinking by controlling your mind switch.

- Deal with your MADs, Green Gorillas and onion layers.

- Fill your own love-cup first.

- Listen to your A mind through hunches and intuition.

- Change your life through positive self-talk.

- Give your way to success.

There are millions of people around the world who, though they overflow with knowledge, continue to be unhappy, unfulfilled, self-sabotaging and unsuccessful. Why?

Few are willing to pay the price for true understanding and wisdom. You can! Use these strategies to unleash The Power Of Positive Doing?

You can create your tomorrows!

As outlined and summarized on the following page, you get back whatever you give out:

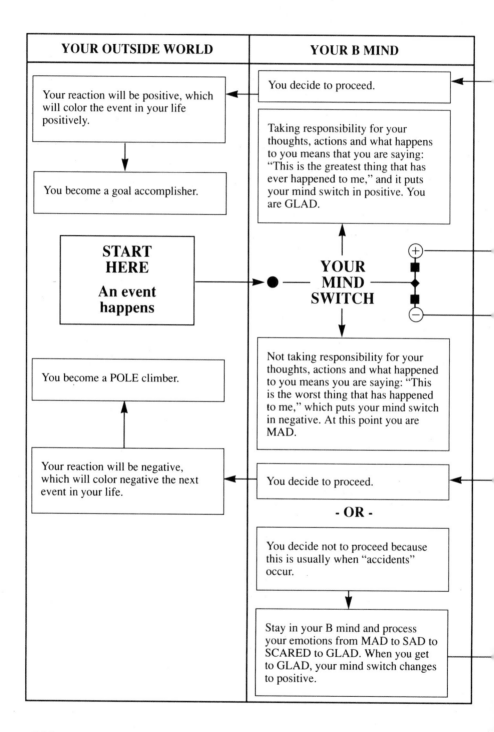

YOUR OUTSIDE WORLD	YOUR B MIND

YOUR OUTSIDE WORLD

Your reaction will be positive, which will color the event in your life positively.

You become a goal accomplisher.

START HERE

An event happens

You become a POLE climber.

Your reaction will be negative, which will color negative the next event in your life.

YOUR B MIND

You decide to proceed.

Taking responsibility for your thoughts, actions and what happens to you means that you are saying: "This is the greatest thing that has ever happened to me," and it puts your mind switch in positive. You are GLAD.

YOUR MIND SWITCH

$\oplus$

$\ominus$

Not taking responsibility for your thoughts, actions and what happened to you means you are saying: "This is the worst thing that has happened to me," which puts your mind switch in negative. At this point you are MAD.

You decide to proceed.

- OR -

You decide not to proceed because this is usually when "accidents" occur.

Stay in your B mind and process your emotions from MAD to SAD to SCARED to GLAD. When you get to GLAD, your mind switch changes to positive.

The Power of Positive Doing

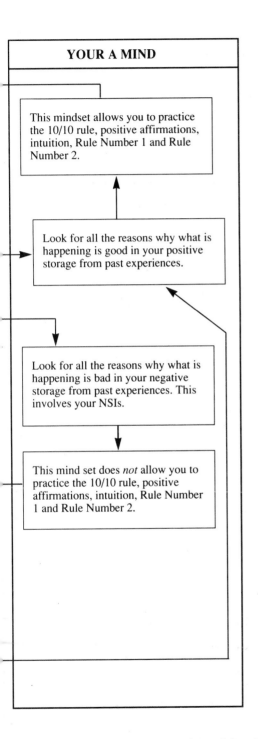

PUTTING

IT

ALL

TOGETHER

A Final Note

Above all, if you want to harvest success, you must first plant it — in your life first, then in the lives of others. You can become a perpetual success machine, especially if you keep returning to the basic foundations.

The secret of success for every person who is, or has ever been successful, lies in the fact that he or she has formed the habit of doing things that failures don't like to do.

What will you do with The Power Of Positive Doing in your life?

Positive +++♥++ Steps

(1) You can create your own success, not just with what you know, but by what you DO!

(2) Few are willing to pay the price for true understanding and wisdom. You can!

(3) Above all, if you want to harvest success, you must first plant it — in your life first, then in the lives of others.

Feed Back

I sincerely hope that you have benefited by reading and applying the tools presented in this book into your life and your environment. I will be delighted to hear from you. Please address all correspondence to International Personal Development, P.O. Box 277, Center Ossipee, N.H. 03814

Ivan G. Burnell

Ivan Burnell has been inspiring people to achieve more than they ever dreamed possible, for the last 30 years. He was born in Brooklyn, N.Y. in 1929, and grew up with an intimate knowledge of the depression and of its effect on peoples' minds. Early in life he joined a family-owned manufacturing business where he was able to use not only his innate engineering skills but also to develop a management style that promoted top quality, timely production work and contented, self confident workers.

After acquiring a degree in engineering, he went on

to other challenges, including a stint as consultant to NASA in preparation for the first manned flight to the moon. Ivan has also worked as chief engineer, insurance agent, farmer, rancher, retail store owner, and vice-president of manufacturing.

In 1978, he started his own company, International Personal Development, and compiled his teachings into a trio of courses called the YES Program. It is a truly effective program. It works. The program has made the lives of many hundreds of people happier and more fulfilled. Those people have been the motivation for the book.

Ivan lives in Center Ossipee, New Hampshire, with his wife Dagny. He teaches the advanced program of YES and develops new teachers for the program. He is also a consultant helping companies develop management techniques that will bring them happy, motivated employees and therefore, successful, profitable businesses.

Notes

Notes

Notes

Notes

Notes

Notes